Managing a Sales Team

Managing a Sales Team
Techniques for Field Sales Managers

Neil R. Sweeney

**Kogan
Page**

First published 1979 in the USA
by Chain Store Publishing Corp,
a subsidiary of Lebhar-Friedman, Inc,
New York

First published 1982 in Great Britain
by Kogan Page Limited,
120 Pentonville Road, London N1
First paperback edition 1987

Copyright © 1979 by Chain Store Publishing Corp

Printed in Great Britain
by Anchor Press, Tiptree, Essex

British Cataloguing in Publication Data

Sweeney, Neil R.
　Managing a sales team: techniques for
　field sales managers.
　1. Sales management
　I. Title
　658.8'1　　HF 5438.4

ISBN 0-85038-539-3
ISBN 1-85091 4885 Paperback

Contents

Preface

This book is about handling or managing people. It does not deal with selling skills; it focuses on the management skills needed to manage sales people. The management style presented is that of a team leader rather than that of overseer.

Because I am a psychologist by training and a trainer by profession, I have presented specific suggestions for handling people throughout this book. These suggestions are the result of my experience working with first-line supervisors over the past thirteen years. They are based on the fact that specific actions and behavior can achieve specific results and reactions. The real test of their applicability, however, is whether they work for you. With this consideration in mind, I have designed the practice exercises and made suggestions to meet individual needs.

I have also made extensive use of examples based on observations and conversations with managers in the consumer product industry. These should help clarify the facts, making them both recognizable and applicable to your specific area.

I have avoided mentioning formal theories of human behavior in my discussion. However, I have used them as a basis for the ideas presented in this book. While such discussions have a place in some books, they do not belong in a book designed to make management simple, interesting, and meaningful. Rather, the topics offered—team building, talking about people, motivating, recruiting, selecting, training, communicating, handling problems, and working with minorities—are geared with a particular goal in mind: to help you improve your ability to be a manager as a result of having read this book.

Should you read this book?

Twelve management tasks and 119 management skills are discussed in this book. The best way to determine whether you should read this book is to rate yourself on each of the management skills discussed.

Management Task #1: Building a Sales Team	Weak	OK	Strong
1. Evaluating the leadership approach required in a given situation.			
2. Using the Take-Charge leadership approach.			
3. Using the Let's-Work-Together leadership approach.			
4. Using the Self-Starter leadership approach.			
5. Determining team mood or morale.			
6. Molding team mood or morale.			
7. Defining roles to be played.			
8. Directing people playing different roles.			
9. Changing roles being played.			
10. Planning and conducting team-oriented meetings.			
11. Designing and carrying out team-oriented contests.			
12. Using team bulletins.			

Management Task #2: Talking About Sales People	Weak	OK	Strong
1. Describing another person's work habits.			

	Weak	OK	Strong
2. Identifying another person's thinking approach.			
3. Describing the way another person relates to others.			
4. Describing another person's emotional makeup.			

Management Task #3:
Motivating Individual Team Members	Weak	OK	Strong
1. Knowing work needs and determining the strength of each team member's work needs.			
2. Determining the way each team member satisfies his needs.			
3. Using the need for pride as a motivator.			
4. Using participation as a motivator.			
5. Using the need to fulfill one's potential as a motivator.			
6. Using the profit need as a motivator.			
7. Using the power need as a motivator.			
8. Using the need for peace as a motivator.			
9. Knowing the individual motivational makeup of each team member.			
10. Determining how an individual team member sees what you want him to do.			
11. Stating what you want an individual team member to do in such a way that it appeals to his makeup and view.			
12. Building a sense of accomplishment in another person.			

Management Task #4:
Recruiting and Selecting Sales People	Weak	OK	Strong
1. Using referrals as a source of people.			
2. Finding people through newspaper ads, agencies, schools, and walk-ins.			
3. Picking up information from an application form.			

	Weak	OK	Strong
4. Determining questions to be asked to clarify information on the application form.			
5. Establishing a conversational tone in the interview.			
6. Getting the applicant talking about himself.			
7. Using test questions to validate skills applicant claims to have.			
8. Interpreting answers to questions asked in an interview.			
9. Explaining the job and building interest in the job.			
10. Getting information regarding work reputation from telephone reference checks.			
11. Interpreting information received from tests.			
12. Sizing up the strengths and weaknesses of a person from the information available.			
13. Determining the risk involved in hiring a person.			
14. Following up on applicants interviewed, but not hired.			

Management Task #5: Group Training

	Weak	OK	Strong
1. Developing discussion topics and questions for group training meetings.			
2. Using questions to get people talking.			
3. Controlling the discussion during the training meeting.			
4. Summarizing discussion during and at the end of the group training meeting.			
5. Introducing, conducting and critiquing role-playing sessions.			
6. Using visuals as group training tools.			

Management Task #6: Individual Training

	Weak	OK	Strong
1. Determining the lesson to be taught.			
2. Organizing the lesson so that it is easier to learn.			

	Weak	OK	Strong
3. Developing training tools to make lessons interesting and relevant.			
4. Adapting the lesson to the learner by using meaningful examples and words.			
5. Explaining a lesson to a learner.			
6. Using training tools.			
7. Using company training programs.			
8. Demonstrating a lesson to a learner.			
9. Rehearsing the learner before he performs.			
10. Observing the learner to determine what he has learned.			
11. Critiquing a learner after observing him.			
12. Making the learner feel rewarded when he learns.			
13. Scheduling training activities.			
14. Following up on the learner to see that he is doing what he was taught.			

Management Task #7:
Evaluating and Improving Performance

	Weak	OK	Strong
1. Developing performance-oriented job descriptions.			
2. Converting the job description to a performance-oriented evaluation form.			
3. Evaluating team members based on performance standards.			
4. Preparing for a performance improvement conference.			
5. Conducting a performance improvement conference.			
6. Getting an individual team member to participate in a discussion of his performance.			
7. Developing a meaningful improvement plan.			
8. Following up on the improvement plan so that improvement actually occurs.			

Management Task #8:
Planning Team Sales Activity

	Weak	OK	Strong
1. Setting sales goals which are specific, measurable, attainable, and compatible.			
2. Developing plans that are based on an accurate evaluation of resources available.			
3. Developing realistic sales strategies for reaching sales goals.			
4. Thinking through plans and converting them to workable schedules.			
5. Pre-planning merchandising oriented, account level, multi-product programs.			
6. Developing meaningful sales forecasts.			
7. Setting appropriate priorities for yourself.			
8. Developing and following personal work schedules.			
9. Organizing information needed for the planning task.			
10. Reconciling the interdependence of plans.			

Management Task #9: Controlling Sales Activities

	Weak	OK	Strong
1. Understanding the management control function.			
2. Using company reports to spot sales problems.			
3. Choosing representative accounts for surveys.			
4. Making meaningful observations of account conditions.			
5. Using industry facts and figures to interpret sales results.			
6. Using information to determine the cause of sales problems.			
7. Developing a solution that helps solve the sales problems.			
8. Developing contingency plans when the original plan fails.			
9. Taking corrective action that leads to sales goals.			
10. Spotting opportunities and taking advantage of them.			

Management Task #10:
Communication with the Sales Team

	Weak	OK	Strong
1. Clarifying what you want to talk about or write about.			
2. Personalizing the message—Names, words, examples.			
3. Anticipating objections and overcoming them.			
4. Stressing key points.			
5. Choosing the best way to send the message.			
6. Getting listeners involved.			
7. Searching for the central message as a listener.			
8. Listening for feeling as well as meaning.			
9. Gaining understanding of written messages by using the SQ3R method.			
10. Giving results producing orders.			
11. Using the telephone appropriately.			
12. Effectively using memos, letters, and message reply forms.			

Management Task #11: Handling People Problems

	Weak	OK	Strong
1. Knowing the rules which deal with your responsibilities to team members and their responsibilities to you.			
2. Determining the rule involved in a grievance or a discipline problem.			
3. Evaluating the applicability of the rule in a specific situation.			
4. Making amends for rules you have broken—grievances.			
5. Imposing meaningful penalities when team members break rules—discipline.			
6. Asking questions to get more information in problems with no known cause.			
7. Using the information to determine the cause.			
8. Developing a solution based on the knowledge of the cause.			
9. Establishing your right to discuss emotionally toned issues.			

	Weak	OK	Strong
10. Stimulating emotional response to what you say.			
11. Developing a solution to an emotionally-toned issue with the person involved.			
12. Battling productively with battlers.			
13. Listening and using complainers.			
14. Using experts to get the job done.			

Management Task #12: Working Productively with Members of Minority Groups

	Weak	OK	Strong
1. Determining the characteristics you associate with minority groups.			
2. Establishing how each person in a minority group differs.			
3. Dealing with individual members of a minority group.			

Acknowledgment

My first memories of the sales world are those of a route sales-man. Working with my father selling bakery products, oleo, coffee, and tea, I developed as an adolescent, some preliminary notions of selling and managing in the consumer products industry. A special thanks to the first salesman I observed, my father, W. Ralph Sweeney.

Many of the sales management ideas presented in this book are the result of my six years experience in training managers for the wine industry at E & J Gallo Winery. A special thanks goes to Dick Witter, Frank Zavell, Ed Schrufer, and Angello Buffalino, sales managers at Gallo, who were simultaneously my teachers and students.

The concepts involved in managing a sales team are most certainly a by-product of sports-oriented sales managers for whom I've worked: Bill Baar, Vice President Sales of Arnold-Oroweat Bakers, Marty Bart, Executive Vice President Sales at Seagram Distillers Company.

There are four sales managers whose perception of their jobs has been so revealing in our discussions of sales management that their contributions to my thinking and to the contents of this book should be noted. They are: Jack Donahue and Barry Stukin of E & J Gallo Winery, Peter Conway, formerly with Proctor and Gamble, now with Gallo, and Sam Taylor of Oroweat.

A final acknowledgment is due to my team, Carole Schilling, my friend, reader, and grammatical consultant and to my two children, Françoise and Patrick, patient observers and enthusiastic supporters.

Chapter 1

Building a Sales Team

"I AM YOUR LEADER"

Whether you are struggling to build a sales team or taking over your first sales team, the role of sales team leader is not yours for the asking. In order to be a functioning leader of a sales team, you must earn the right to lead the people on your team.

In the royal tradition of the past, a person became king when the crown was placed on his head. Our own democratic tradition makes a person a leader following an election. Sales teams are a little different. Sales organizations are existing, functioning organizations in which the role of leader can be played by team members as well as by the designated leader. Clearly, being a team leader means more than having the title: Sales Manager.

This chapter on building a sales team discusses the skills a leader needs: knowledge of leadership styles, skill in defining roles and the ability to use team mood. Also discussed are the team-building activities: participative meetings, team bulletins and contests.

ALL FOR ONE AND ONE FOR ALL

Many groups of people call themselves teams when they are not as a matter of fact teams. A group of people who work toward a common goal but work independently cannot rightfully be called a team. A group of people who do things but do them without some type of guiding direction cannot be called a team; there is no leader.

> A *team* consists of a group of people with a common goal who work interdependently with defined yet varying roles and work under a recognized leader who directs team activities and controls team morale.

A sales team is a group of people who work with each other, cooperate with each other and help each other to reach sales goals. The idea behind a team could not be more simple: All for one and one for all. The process of building a sales team, however, is a bit more complex.

The person who determines whether and how a group of people will work together is the leader or manager of the group. How he leads has an enormous impact on the success of the team. His *leadership style* and his skill in sensing and molding loyalties and needs are all-important. They affect the feeling that team members have toward their group. This feeling is called *team mood*. If you don't learn how to deal with the mood of the group, building a team is difficult.

Teams are built on cooperation and interdependence. This requires that every member understand and accept the roles of the other people in the group. The ability to *define the roles* of each member and to change roles when necessary is a key team-building skill. While business interaction may seem obvious to you, members of the same work group often perform their own jobs independently without recognizing how their job contributes to goals of the team. Your job is to build teamwork and commitment through helping them recognize their contributions and how they affect group goals.

YOUR INSTRUCTIONS: BUILD A TEAM

You have just been assigned a position as a sales manager for a new team. The salespeople on your team are:

Martha Jones—age 24. Martha has the smallest sales territory on the team and just recently started with the company. Because she is new and did not have sales experience before she joined the company, she is still an unknown producer. The retailers she calls on are not sure she knows what she is doing and tend to call in more orders than they give her. Her appearance reflects her former profession—modeling.

Frank Bartelli—age 34. Frank is one of the more cooperative members of the team. He is known for his willingness to help others when they have a difficult sales problem to solve. He does well in his own territory, but he is not the biggest earner on the team. It's more important to him to be well liked than it is to earn a lot of money. He's already making more money than he ever did as a teacher.

Henry White—age 38. Henry is noted for his frankness. He lets everybody know he knows his business. His retailers respect him even if they don't like him. He considers most bosses as unnecessary nuisances. The only manager he has a good word for is his first boss who, he says, "taught him everything he needed to learn about the business." Before joining the sales organization, he was a very successful insurance salesperson.

Arthur Anderson—age 31. Arthur wins every contest. He's a team player for sure. A professional ex-athlete, he claims that a person who hasn't played competitive sports just can't learn how to sell. It's difficult for him to understand indifference and lack of productivity. His favorite role is backup man for the boss.

Manuel Rodriquez—age 26. Manuel is great with his retailers. They regard him as a conscientious salesperson who always has their interests at heart. He's a former radio announcer who enjoys making speeches and talking to people one at a time. In a group, he clams up, seldom says a word. He's a good producer for sure but not one to set the world on fire.

Carl Volmer—age 46. Carl likes to run his own show. Carl prides himself on knowing the accounts in his territory better than anybody. He has doubled his income in the last two years. As a former sales manager, he feels he knows in-store merchandising as well as managing. Although Carl sometimes works in spurts, he generally reaches his sales and merchandising goals.

This group of people, diverse as it is, can be molded into a team using the team-building skills outlined below:

Team-building skills for field sales managers:

- Lead with skill and sensitivity
- Be able to sense and mold team mood
- Define and change roles when necessary
- Develop commitment to team goals

HOW TO LEAD

A successful team leader knows how to get people to follow him. Many managers try to find the one best possible method of managing. However, the most successful leaders use different approaches in different situations and with different people. Martha, for example, needs a great deal of firm guidance and reassurance. She wants to feel that she can count on your support. Manuel, on the other hand, needs to feel a sense of independence and responsibility for his work. You should give him relative freedom in handling his territory while you make it clear that he can get help if he needs it. In these two situations, clearly, two different approaches are necessary: a firm hand with Martha; tolerance and flexibility with Manuel. As long as you yourself are sensitive to the approach necessary, you will be both successful and effective as a leader and manager.

THREE LEADERSHIP APPROACHES

Basically, there are three leadership approaches or styles of leading. These include: 1) the "take charge" approach, 2) the "let's work together" approach, and 3) the "self-starter" approach. Each of these leadership approaches is effective in working with some people and ineffective in working with others. Consequently, a team leader must learn how and when to use each. Or, to state it another way, there are times to act like a Prussian general, like the president of the PTA, or like the chairman of the board. By knowing when and with whom to use each approach, you will be a more effective and successful sales manager.

The "Take Charge" Approach

With the "take charge" style, the manager is the center of all activity and tends to make most of the decisions. He makes plans, sees that they are implemented and solves any problems that arise. He tells people what to do, how to do it and in how much time. Since he gives commands, obedience is required.

Since insecure and untrained people usually look to their superiors for firm direction, the "take charge" style is effective with this type of salesperson. Because of inexperience or uncertainty, some salespeople need to have decisions made for them until either they learn the job or they become more sure of themselves. When employees act like this, the "take charge" approach is generally best.

Take Charge Leader:
1. Very little trust
2. Takes responsibility personally
3. Determines goals
4. Tracks closely—catch them
5. Results or else
6. Demands obedience
7. Personally rewards and punishes
8. Leader solves problems alone or finds a scapegoat

The "Let's Work Together" Approach

The "let's work together" style is more democratic than the "take charge" approach. Here, the manager is responsible for stimulating and directing activities. The team is the center of all activity. He sets sales goals with the involvement of team members and develops plans with the help of team members. He checks to be sure that plans are implemented successfully, involves the group in problem solving, and offers help and direction when the team goals are not being reached. Since this is a style that relies on interdependence, cooperation is a "must."

More experienced salespeople and those with a strong commitment to the sales organization for which they work respond well to this approach. With salespeople who are interested in their work, and who enjoy working and cooperating with others, the "let's work together" approach is an effective one.

WORK TOGETHER LEADER
1. Some trust, but not total trust
2. Shares responsibility
3. Suggests goals
4. Periodically checks—discovers overlooked goals
5. Results through team
6. Builds on cooperation
7. Uses group to reward and punish
8. Leader solves problems with the group

The "Self-Starter" Approach

Some employees, however, are not only highly competent and uniquely skilled, but highly self-motivated as well. These are people with initiative and self-starting energy who get particular enjoyment in working by themselves and in solving problems alone.

With this kind of salesperson, a manager merely has to give the go-ahead and he'll be on his way. That is the heart of the "self-starter" leadership style. With a clear understanding of what this individual can and cannot do, the manager can give him free rein in the territory to plan and carry out sales and merchandising programs. The manager simply requires that the salesperson be committed to the team goals. Without such commitment, this approach will be ineffective.

SELF-STARTER LEADER

1. Total trust in individuals
2. Allows individual responsibility
3. Lets individuals set goals
4. Gets commitment—reviews goal attainment
5. Individual results
6. Encourages initiative
7. Depends on self-reward and punishment
8. Individual members solve, leader assists if needed

WHAT APPROACH TO USE WITH YOUR TEAM MEMBERS

Let's return to the team members and consider which approaches will work best for which members. Uncertain Martha clearly needs a sense of support and of firm direction: the "take charge" style would probably be best for her. It is probably in order for Henry too, since he falls into the category of employee who works best when his aggression is channeled by a firm hand.

Frank is an experienced worker who particularly enjoys helping and sharing his successes and problems with his fellow sales representatives. While he is quite independent, he would obviously feel deprived working alone. Therefore, take the "let's work together" approach with him. While not so keen on helping others, Arthur likes the challenge of being top salesperson all the time. He also would respond well to the "let's work together" style.

The "self-starter" style would work best with Manuel and Carl. Both are competent self-starters who like to run their own territories. While Carl is more sociable than Manuel, they both know how to sell.

Both of these people do best without interference, enjoy working alone and have enough initiative and self-motivation to handle the job alone. You should feel comfortable giving each of them free rein.

Leadership Approach and the Individual

While there are no hard and fast rules for leading people, the following recommendations seem to make sense in terms of the type of role a sales representative or group is playing:

Use "take charge" approach with:

> *The Hostile Sales Representative.* He resents authority. He's an angry person. Yet, his hostility must be met by a show of authority. The autocratic approach has the effect of channeling aggressiveness, confining his energies to constructive ends.

> *The Insecure Sales Representative.* This type of person feels the need for firm rule. His sense of dependence gives him a feeling of being at loose ends, up in the air unless the leader is authoritative and dominant. Firm guidance gives him reassurance.

Use "let's work together" approach with:

> *The Cooperative Sales Representative.* This person is not necessarily unaggressive. But his aggressiveness, unlike that of hostile individuals, takes constructive paths. The cooperative-aggressive individual will head in the right direction with minimum control.

The Group-Minded Sales Representative. The individual who enjoys "team play" will probably function best if your approach to him is "let's work together." He has less need for direction, since he regards his work essentially as a *group* job. He finds his greatest satisfaction in a friendly, closely knit group.

Use the "self-starter" approach with:

The Individualistic Sales Representative. He is usually most productive under the free-rein type of leadership if he knows his job. Even if he tends to be a show-off, a "grandstand player," let him have his head, unless considerations of group welfare or resentments of other individuals give you cause to modify your approach.

The Loner Salesman. Whether you call them introverts or describe them as "withdrawn," some people have an aversion to dealing with more than one person at a time.
Such individuals are likely to do their best work on their own. The atmosphere created by the "self-starter" approach is most conducive to their peace of mind, most relaxed and effective effort.

PRACTICE EXERCISE: Team Leadership

In order to apply what you have learned about team leadership, think about the people who report to you and answer the questions below.

1. List the five members of your team and identify the leadership approach you would use with each of them.

Name	Brief Description	"Take Charge"	"Work Together"	"Self-Starter"

2. Which of the leadership approaches seems most difficult for you?

_____

What reasons can you give for this? _____

_____

_____

Discuss this approach with your boss and try using it when appropriate during the coming week.

SENSE AND MOLD TEAM MOOD

The mood is tense. The mood is cheerful. The mood is hopeful. The mood is angry. All of these statements can be made about work teams at times. A manager should be able to detect team mood and to mold it. These are skills that are particularly difficult to learn and to build, because they deal with emotions or feelings, yours and the group's.

Team mood is the feeling team members have toward their group. It is also sometimes called morale. Team mood results from feelings accumulated day after day. A group of salespeople experiencing continual frustration and conflict will accumulate negative feelings that will cause low morale. Feelings like this in turn foster poor performance as well as a lack of commitment and involvement. People who feel satisfied and proud to be a part of their team usually experience a minimum of conflict. Their positive mood or high morale generally means that they take an interest in their jobs and enjoy their work.

To create a positive mood, you should establish a feeling of success. This is accomplished first by assigning or agreeing to goals that each salesperson can realistically handle. In addition, it's important that you express your appreciation for their accomplishments. This will help to reinforce their success and pride in their job.

Team moods frequently take their tone from your own feelings. You yourself are a mood setter. If you don't like your job and feel frustrated, the people who work for you may sense this feeling, which can be communicated in even the subtlest ways. A sense of enthusiasm and encouragement, on the other hand, is also contagious. You should recognize, therefore, that one of the major contributions to team mood is directly under your control—your own feelings.

Another important factor in team mood is the way you deal with emotionally toned issues. The way you respond to personal tragedies in the lives of your salespeople, how you terminate or demote an employee, your handling of an explosive issue, all will influence the mood of your team.

A cold, inhuman attitude may be efficient, but it also builds up resentment and anger that result in a nonproductive group. Terminating unpleasant Ursula, the rude sales demonstrator who has been on the team for the last four years, is a delicate deed. However, you must find a way to handle it with human kindness. Remember: The way you handle the emotionally toned issues of one employee can set the mood for the entire group. One of the most effective ways to detect team mood is to pay attention to the behavior of the group. Loud protests or sudden tears suggest that the group as a whole is tense. Smiling faces and cheery "hellos," on the other hand, suggest a more cheerful state of affairs. By observing the expressions and behavior of the people who work for you, you can detect individual and group moods. This will help you to recognize and continue positive responses or do something about whatever problems or dissatisfactions exist.

DEFINE AND CHANGE ROLES WHEN NECESSARY

In order for a team to work effectively, each member of the team must accept and play a designated role. Assigned work roles are usually stated in job descriptions; actual roles and social roles are discovered on the job. The difference between assigned and actual roles depends upon the salesperson himself, his boss, the support staff and his customers.

The assigned work role of a field sales representative may be to sell merchandising ideas that sell cases to consumers. Because of the sales representative's personal desire for a big commission check and his distaste for the thinking required to sell merchandising ideas, his actual role may be that of solicitor and order taker. If his boss measures only cases sold and does not survey in-store conditions in the sales representative's territory, he is in effect re-inforcing the changed role.

The first role that must be defined on a team is the manager's role. Your job description says you perform certain tasks and handle certain responsibilities. What do you actually do? What is your social role in the group? The relief man? The bill collector? The negotiator? The scapegoat? So long as that role does not restrict your activities, interfere with your leadership effectiveness or discourage employee morale, it does not need to be changed. Only when the role you play interferes with team goals is it time to re-examine the situation for alternative forms of behavior.

The job description that states assigned work roles is a good place to begin to define the actual work roles and social roles of each team member. What is each salesperson supposed to be doing? What is he actually doing?

Like your role, if the actual role and the social role do not interfere with territory and team goals, they do not need to be changed. A sales representative who is still tracking by hand what the computer now tracks for him need not change until this practice starts to interfere with his effectiveness. As long as a sales representative can handle retail accounts and headquarter accounts without neglecting either, his work role can remain unchanged.

An important point to keep in mind about social roles is that groups of different rather than similar people add interest and variety to work. A team often works best, in fact, with varying social roles. There should be room on every team for the critic, the joker, the fireball, the "yes" man and the "no sir."

If you find a team member playing an informal group leader, he may be an important key to communicating with the group. You might want to sound out ideas with him first before putting them into effect for the entire group. Or, he may be willing to explain your point of view to others or to explain the group's feelings to you. Through his social role, he may be an important means of helping you manage and influence others in the group. In this capacity, his social role can be an important factor in keeping communication lines open.

Your job as team leader is to define roles and use the roles to the team's best advantage. Definition of actual and social roles and the ability to change them when necessary is a team-building skill that can be yours to use with effectiveness and success if you are aware of their possibilities.

PRACTICE EXERCISE: Developing a Role Definition

Take a look at the roles being played by two of your sales representatives with the same job description.

How do their actual roles differ? _____

_____

_____

How are their actual roles similar? _____

_____

_____

State below how you think the sales representatives you have trained will perform their jobs differently than those trained by other managers.

_____

_____

_____

_____

How do you think the role of the sales representatives on your team would change if you suddenly doubled the number of products they have to sell and merchandise?

_____

_____

_____

BUILDING COMMITMENT TO TEAM GOALS

The goals of a football team are clear and the interaction between team members obviously necessary. Sales team goals are less obviously dependent on interaction. Each sales representative has his own territory and he is responsible for reaching sales and merchandising goals in that territory. It is true that the success or failure of a team is the result of the activities of salespeople in each territory, but what is the sales representative's involvement with others? On some occasions, special problems develop in one territory that make it impossible for the sales rep to reach goals; these goals must be offset by increased productivity in other territories. Vacancies occur in sales teams and that means someone must cover the territories; if the manager does it, he will not be able to give the backup to his people that they normally depend on. Like all organizations, a sales team must involve commitment to team goals. Building commitment to team goals can be accomplished by conducting participative meetings, having team oriented contests and issuing team bulletins.

Conducting Participative Team Meetings

Meetings which permit salespeople to get involved build commitment to team goals. Common problems and available opportunities can be discussed by all members of the team and solutions and plans of action developed. Meetings which are called to collect reports and deliver ultimatums are not the kind of meetings which build commitment to the team goals. This type of meeting discourages participation and reinforces the attitude of every person for himself. Participative meetings do not occur by chance, they require planning.

Successful participative meetings require more thought than jotting down some notes a few minutes before the meeting begins. Topics to be discussed and methods of getting team members involved must be decided well in advance. The timing for each topic must be established and the order in which topics are to be covered must be decided.

There are many ways of getting team members involved in a discussion of topics. Some examples are: assigning a team member to make a presentation on a topic which is then discussed, viewing and discussing a movie, asking all of the team members to read an article and then discuss it, role playing a sales pitch. The key element in all of these is participation—the team members have a chance to talk about something they read, hear about or see. This involvement builds commitment to team goals.

PRACTICE EXERCISE: Planning a Participative Team Meeting

From the information presented below, prepare a meeting agenda.

DATE:	Thursday, June 15 or Friday, June 16
LOCATION:	Sales office or Dix Hotel
TIME:	2 P.M. or 3 P.M. start (approximately 2 hours)
TO ATTEND:	All salespeople on team (6)
	Your Boss—General Sales Manager
	You—Sales Manager
	Mary Kline—Order Clerk
SUBJECTS:	A. Show the ad for the new product.
	B. Review team sales and merchandising accomplishments in last two weeks.
	C. Explain new order form and use.
	D. Provide some type of training for the salespeople on "Handling Objections."
	E. Discuss problem of getting floor displays for the new product.

OTHER MEETING FACTORS:

Mary Kline must leave meeting promptly at 4 P.M. to accept late afternoon orders.

A 10- or 15-minute coffee break.

Your boss wants something added to the meeting to provide a strong opening and closing.

Your boss wants some answers to the problem of floors for new product.

You want to maximize participation in the meeting.

MEETING AGENDA FORM

LOCATION: _____ DATE: _____

START MEETING: _____

SEATING ARRANGEMENT: _____

MEETING THEME: _____

DETAILED AGENDA:

TOPIC	TECHNIQUE	SPECIFIC TIME	VISUAL AIDS/ PROPS/PASSOUTS

Team Oriented Contests

The second way commitment to team goals can be gained is by the use of team oriented contests. This type of contest rewards team achievement as well as achievement by individual team members. Team oriented contests have team goals as well as territory goals; there are no winners unless the team wins. This encourages interaction and stimulates interest in the success of other team members.

Like all contests, team oriented contests should:

- Be based on records which all of the sales representatives trust.
- Give every team and every member of the team an equal opportunity to win.
- Have an appealing incentive.
- Be explained in full before the contest begins.

The best incentives for sales contests are guilt-free luxuries: something that the sales representative would like to have but probably would not buy because it is really not essential.

Bulletins as Team Builders

Team bulletins keep every member of the team informed. Whether they are issued weekly, bi-weekly or once a month, the sales and merchandising goals reached by each member of the team are in clear sight. This gives the team members who are reaching their goals an opportunity to explain how they succeeded. Team bulletins encourage team members to help each other and allows other members to benefit from success of individual team members. Greater commitment to team goal results.

SUMMARY: WHAT A TEAM IS ALL ABOUT

A sales team is a group of people who have a common goal who work interdependently with defined yet varying roles and work under a recognized leader who directs team activities and controls team morale.

You will know that you have a team when you and your people begin to speak and act like a team. Words like "we," "us" and "our" will be frequently in your vocabulary. Team members will trust each other, depend on each other, give to each other, take from each other and cooperate with each other. The benefit to all of you is a more productive, efficient and satisfied group.

Building a team does not come about just by having people responsible to you, giving them assignments and waiting for results. Team building requires time, skill and team-oriented activities. Recognizing the importance and significance of building a cooperative, interdependent team will help you be a more effective, productive and successful manager.

QUESTIONS THAT NEED ANSWERS

To be sure that you understand the ideas discussed in this chapter, answer the following questions.

1. One of the major differences between team members and members of a work group is that team members:
   a) do their jobs well.
   b) help each other.
   c) respect authority.
   d) know what to do.

2. The "take charge" leadership approach:
   a) doesn't work all of the time.
   b) is effective with insecure people.
   c) requires obedience.
   d) all of these.

3. Loners respond best to which of the following leadership approaches:
   a) "take charge."
   b) "self-starter."
   c) "let's work together."
   d) can't say.

4. In order to be an effective team leader, a manager must be able to use:
   a) all three leadership approaches.
   b) the "take charge" approach.
   c) the "let's work together" approach.
   d) the "self-starter" approach.

5. Morale is another word for:
   a) team mood.
   b) high productivity.
   c) fickle feelings.
   d) job awareness.

6. Job descriptions:
   a) rule out role confusion.
   b) specify how things are to be done.
   c) indicate who is boss.
   d) outline roles to be played.

7. Commitment to team goals can be built by:
   a) holding team meetings.
   b) posting the goals on the bulletin board.
   c) outlining team goals to your boss.
   d) letting members know the score.

8. Easel pads or flip charts can be used at meetings to:
   a) tell a joke.
   b) outline key points.
   c) replace passouts.
   d) present new forms.

9. All contests:
   a) build team spirit.
   b) cause friction.
   c) make everybody work harder.
   d) none of these.

10. The words "we," "us" and "our" suggest that the work group:
    a) needs somebody to take charge.
    b) is a team.
    c) has abandoned the leader.
    d) is close.

If you made the following choices, you should feel that the ideas discussed are yours: 1b, 2d, 3b, 4a, 5a, 6d, 7d, 8b, 9d, 10b.

Chapter 2

Talking about People

IT'S LIKE TALKING ABOUT YOURSELF

How can you describe another person? He is either a good person or a bad person. He is either cooperative or uncooperative. These descriptions are short and are very general. So let's add another possibility: He's either an extrovert or an introvert. Now our description is a bit more complex, but not much more substantive. Many managers are lost for words when it comes to meaningfully describing other people. Perhaps this is because the childhood prohibition against talking about others has lasted into adulthood, even when it is important to do so. In fact, most people find that describing people is as difficult as describing themselves.

The best way to develop your skill in talking about people is to list all of the words you can think of to describe a person. Then you can convert these words into a rating form.

WHY DESCRIBE PEOPLE?

Why should a field sales manager be interested in developing the skills needed to describe people? Until a field sales manager learns to evaluate the qualities of others, his chances of handling them successfully are lowered. If you can't evaluate the kind of person who makes a good salesperson, you may not know how to find one. Since describing people comes first in building people handling skills, let's look at some important descriptive words.

WORDS AND WORD CATEGORIES

What does a field sales manager need to know about a person in order to work productively with him? While the list of important characteristics could be endless, experience has shown that just 24 words can describe a person's most important attributes.

To make the task even simpler, each of these words can be grouped into one of four categories. The first category of words deals with a person's approach to his work. One of the words in this category is lazy; another, efficient. The second category deals with the kind of thinker a person is. Words like smart or flexible fall into this category. What a person is like when dealing with others is the third category. Shy, tactful, or aggressive are some possibilities. The fourth category describes the emotional outlook of a person. He may be cheerful, irritable or self-assured. The four categories of words in brief are: work approach, thinking approach, dealing with others, and emotional outlook, or simply: work, thinking, with others, and emotions.

Before the Peopleometer is introduced, two more ideas should be noted. First, every word has an opposite. The opposite of lazy is energetic. The opposite of aggressive is passive. This means that the 24 words can become 48 if their opposites are used and this allows a greater range of possibilities. Second, characteristics can be quantified when they are used to describe people. That is, people can be more or less lazy. A person can be rated and found to be not only either blunt or tactful, but somewhere in between. If you use a line to connect the two words, you can indicate where on the line a person is:

BLUNT ———————————|————————— TACTFUL

THE PEOPLEOMETER
A Rating Chart to Use in Describing a Person

1. What is his approach to work?

LAZY ————————|————————	ENERGETIC
PERSISTENT ——————|—————	EASILY DISCOURAGED
RESPONSIBLE ——————|————	UNDEPENDABLE
SELF-STARTING ————|————	NEEDFUL OF ORDERS
EFFICIENT ——————|—————	INEFFICIENT
SLOW ————————|————	FAST
PUTS OFF ————————|——	PROMPT

2. What kind of thinker is he?

QUICK ——————|————————	SLOW
DULL ——————|————————	SMART
ABSTRACT ————|——————	PRACTICAL
FLEXIBLE ——————|—————	RIGID
ACCEPTING ————|——————	CRITICAL
PLANFUL ——————|————	IMPULSIVE
LOOKS AT WHOLE ——|———	FOCUSES ON DETAILS
INDEPENDENT ————|———	CONFORMIST

3. What is he like with other people?

SOCIABLE ————|——————	SHY
BLUNT ——————|—————	TACTFUL
A FOLLOWER ————|————	A LEADER
AGGRESSIVE ————|————	PASSIVE
COOPERATIVE ————|———	OPPOSITIONAL

4. What is he like emotionally?

GLOOMY ————————|———	CHEERFUL
IRRITABLE ——————|———	EASY-GOING
EASILY HURT ————|———	TOUGH
SELF-ASSURED ————|——	INSECURE

DEFINITION OF EACH OF THE WORDS USED

In making up the Peopleometer, words that have the greatest meaning for most field sales managers were used. While most people know what the words mean, a definition of each of the words is given below to insure clarity and to provide a reference should confusion arise.

Approach to work:

Lazy: Doesn't enjoy working and spends considerable time and effort avoiding it. Takes life easy.

Energetic: Enjoys being busy and finds work to do even when not under pressure.

Persistent: Approaches work tasks with determination. Sticks with a job until it is done, no matter how difficult.

Easily discouraged: Gets things done as long as things go well and no difficulties develop. If difficulties develop, turns to something else.

Responsible: Can be depended upon to do his part. Takes his work seriously. Accepts responsibility for doing his share.

Undependable: Makes light of work responsibilities. Seems to say, "If I don't do it, someone else will." Can't be depended upon.

Self-starting: Once he knows what is expected of him, will initiate work for himself. Takes the initiative.

Needful of orders: Although he may know what is expected, he waits for someone else to tell him what to do. Waits for work and seldom does things without being told to do them.

Efficient: His efforts lead to results. Wasted time and effort are kept at a minimum.

Inefficient: May keep busy, but never seems to get anything accomplished. Lots of wasted time and motion.

Slow: Does not keep up with the work pace of others who do the same job.

Fast: Works faster than others who do the same or similar jobs.

Puts off: While aware of the importance of work tasks, tends to delay doing them until either it is too late or he must push himself extraordinarily hard to get them done on time.

Prompt: Likes to get things done without delay. Seldom puts off until tomorrow what he can do today.

What kind of thinker the person is:

Quick: Catches on to things fast. Seems to gain an understanding of things after brief exposure to the relevant information.

Slow: Takes a long time to learn things. Only understands something after repeated actions or explanations.

Dull: Not knowledgeable in relevant areas. Seems to have difficulty learning.

Smart: Seems to be informed in many areas, and demonstrates a superior ability to learn.

Abstract: Interested in ideas that are abstract or speculative. Likes to deal with theoretical concepts.

Practical: Interested in ideas that lead to practical results. Likes to discuss practical problems and solutions.

Flexible: Sees things in relative terms—shades of gray rather than black or white. Has opinions that can be changed through persuasive argument or discussion.

Rigid: Sees things as absolutes, either black or white. Vehemently resists changing his opinions.

Accepting: Tends to accept information and statements at face value. Typically does not question or examine things critically.

Critical: Questions information provided by others. Examines statements made by others carefully and critically.

Planful: Thinks things through before doing them. Sees the future implications of his decisions and their impact on others.

Impulsive: Acts without thinking things through. Frequently embarrassed by not having considered the results of the decisions he makes.

Looks at whole: Tries to organize information first. After understanding the whole, he can explain the parts.

Focuses on details: Takes information apart before he can put it together. Looks first at the detail and then the whole picture.

Independent: Tends to look at things independent of other people. Comes up with new ideas and thinks in terms of change.

Conformist: Frequently looks at things as most of the people he knows looks at them. Understands the status quo but rarely comes up with new or innovative ideas.

What is the person like with other people:

Sociable: Likes to be with other people, and enjoys doing things with others. Relaxed when he is with others.

Shy: Generally keeps to himself. Often does things by himself rather than with other people.

Blunt: Says things directly to people without cushioning the impact. Sometimes lacks tact.

Tactful: Says even critical things in such a way that other people are not usually offended. Shows concern about not hurting other people's feelings.

A Follower: Looks to others to tell him what to do. Prefers to allow others to make important decisions.

A Leader: Likes to take charge. Enjoys the responsibility of making decisions for other people as well as for himself. Often resists others who try to tell him what to do.

Aggressive: Enjoys challenging people and ideas. Often attacks contrary points of view and rarely backs down when threatened. May even fight if necessary.

Passive: Prefers not to be in conflict with others. Lets things go by rather than arguing contrary points of view. Backs down when threatened.

Cooperative: Willing to go along with others. Will adjust to reasonable demands of others.

Oppositional: Likes things his own way. Has difficulty going along with others.

What is the person like emotionally:

Gloomy: Always down in the dumps. Characteristically depressed and usually in a bad or sad mood.

Cheerful: Easy-going and generally happy. Usually makes others happy when is around them. Tends to hide gloomy moments.

Irritable: Easily angered. Irked often by many things. Inclined to blow his top in times of stress.

Easy-going: Not easily upset or angered. Keeps control of his feelings even in times of stress.

Easily hurt: Particularly sensitive to criticism, and often takes well-meant comments as criticism. Takes even small things hard.

Tough: Feels self-confident and rolls with the punches. Is not easily hurt, and can take criticism well without falling to pieces.

Self-assured: Has confidence in himself. Feels that he can do most things well or adequately and usually does.

Insecure: Lacks confidence in himself. Needs reassurance often to be sure that he is doing things well.

THE USEFULNESS OF THE PEOPLEOMETER

After you have evaluated a team member in terms of the Peopleometer scale, you will discover how detailed your evaluation will be. For example, if you are asked about a particular individual, your first impulse may be to say, "He's a good man who works hard and is very reliable." After evaluating him in terms of the Peopleometer, however, your comments may be something like this: "He is smart, practical, relatively rigid, critical, and generally conforming. Nevertheless, he is energetic, persistent, generally responsible, and fast, although not particularly efficient. He also tends to be a follower by nature and rather shy, but he can lead when necessary. He's neither aggressive nor passive, but right in between. While he is too easily irritated and hurt and needs frequent reassurance, still he maintains a cheerful outlook when he feels that he is making sales."

Obviously, the second description is far more detailed than the first and will be of far greater help in working with an individual. Through continued use of the Peopleometer, you should gain facility in offering evaluations and ease in talking about those evaluations.

BUILDING SKILLS IN DESCRIBING PEOPLE

One of the chief advantages of the Peopleometer is its simplicity. This should help you to refine your skills so that you can evaluate people more easily and talk more meaningfully about them.

You might start by using the Peopleometer to rate yourself. Then ask someone who knows you well to rate you. Or if it's easier, rate a third person you both know. Compare your ratings and discuss them if there is a disagreement about the meanings of the words. Learning to talk about other people takes practice. The more you do it, the easier it will become.

PRACTICE EXERCISE: Describing Salespeople

Using the Peopleometer rate the best and the worst sales representative who works for you, according to each of the four categories.

Best Sales Representative:

Work: _____

Thinking: _____

With Others: _____

Emotions: _____

Worst Sales Representative:

Work: _____

Thinking: _____

With Others: _____

Emotions: _____

The words that you have used to evaluate these two people should make it possible for you to see the differences and similarities between them. From there, it will enable you to talk meaningfully about them.

What are the key words that demonstrate the main differences between the worst and the best sales representative?

SUMMARY: AVOID GOSSIP

This chapter is designed to help you refine your skills of evaluating and describing people. It should help give you the words and categories to evaluate more effectively a person's approach to work, his thinking approach, his manner of dealing with others, and his emotional makeup. Your evaluation should be based on what you yourself know and see of him.

Be very careful, however, to avoid prejudicing your evaluation or your handling of people on the basis of what other people say. Unless you have evidence beyond a reasonable doubt that your evaluation is incorrect, proceed with your own observations. In general, by basing the way you handle people on what you yourself know about them, you will be a more objective and more effective manager.

QUESTIONS THAT NEED ANSWERS

To be sure that you understand the ideas discussed in this chapter, answer the following questions.

1. The Peopleometer contains:
   a) 24 descriptive words.
   b) 3 categories of words.
   c) 48 descriptive words.
   d) 24 categories of words.

2. "He can be depended upon to do his part" is a definition for which of the following words:
   a) self-starter.
   b) efficient.
   c) fast.
   d) responsible.

3. The four things you should know about a person are represented by which of the following groups of words:
   a) work, feelings, personality, thinking.
   b) energetic, smart, shy, somber.
   c) work, thinking, with others, emotions.
   d) personality, energy, training, structure.

4. Tactful is a word used to describe how a person:
   a) works.
   b) deals with people.
   c) feels.
   d) perceives information.

5. The Peopleometer enables you to:
   a) make quantitative judgments.
   b) rate opposites.
   c) speak meaningfully of others.
   d) all of these.

If you made the following choices, you should feel that the ideas are yours: 1c, 2d, 3c, 4b, 5d.

Chapter 3

Motivating a Sales Team

"SALES PEOPLE ARE LIKE MULES"

There is an old saying that "salespeople are like mules, you can motivate them with a carrot or a club." The club being a threatening object to be avoided and the carrot an appealing reward to be sought. Having spent many hours observing managers trying to motivate others, it would seem to me that the saying pretty well sums up motivation—that is, if you remember that carrots and clubs move people and mules only if they are hungry and fearful. If we stopped discussing motivation at this point, we would have to define the manager's job as a motivator in these words: Master of Fear and Dispenser of Goodies.

WHAT ARE WE TALKING ABOUT?

Motivation has to do with the ways a manager uses to get people to do what he wants them to do. The word *motive*, or *need*, can be defined as a force within a person that moves a person into action. One type of motive is called a physical motive, e.g. hunger. The other type of motive is called a psychological motive, e.g. participation. A person who is hungry will seek food. A person who has a need to participate and is not involved will seek out opportunities to participate. Motivation is based on the idea that if you know why people do things, you can get them to do what you want them to do.

EVERY MANAGER MOTIVATES!

Because most of our training is product knowledge or sales-skill oriented rather than management oriented, many people are awed by the idea that they have to motivate people who work for them. When you come to think about it, it is a foreboding thing to have the responsibility of getting all kinds of people—young and old, male and female—to do what you want them to do. Structured this way, it is no wonder that many managers prefer to put off thoughtful consideration of motivation. Unfortunately, this is not possible. One way or another every manager motivates. While some managers are more effective than others, as long as a manager gives an order and has it followed, as long as one sales representative is helped to reach a sales goal thought impossible, the manager has motivated. To be a manager is to motivate.

IMPROVING YOUR SKILL AS A MOTIVATOR

Earlier we suggested that the manager motivates by instilling fear and dispensing goodies. It should be remembered that the use of fear is effective as long as the people you manage can be threatened and you know how to instill fear without destroying those you threaten. Classic leadership models from fathers to generals to police officers all know how to instill fear and as a result get people to do what they want them to do. The first way to improve your skill as a motivator is to learn to *instill productive fear*. But what of this skill, dispenser of goodies? Certainly we are not speaking of the manager as a Santa Claus, although I understand that he can be used quite effectively at Christmas time to get children to behave. What we are saying is: A manager must learn to present and control work tasks and work rewards in such a way that the people will gain the rewards and the satisfactions they seek from work.

What are people trying to get out of work?

The most obvious answer is a paycheck. Gaining personal profit has to be one of the major needs satisfied by work. There are, however, some other important things that people seek from their work.

Psychologists such as Maslow and Schneiders have developed extensive lists of needs. Unfortunately, they do not lend themselves to easy use in the work world. Rather than present these lists, let's consider a more useable list of needs developed in response to the question, "What do you want from work besides a paycheck?" The most frequent answers were:

1. "An opportunity to do my own thing. An opportunity to achieve something, to be somebody, to receive some recognition for what I can do."

2. "A chance to direct and help others. I enjoy *controlling* other people."

3. "To be a *part* of a group. A chance to participate in productive work efforts with other people."

4. "A chance to use my talents and make myself better. An opportunity to grow and develop, to fulfill my *potential*."

Does this make sense in terms of the salespeople who work for you? Pride? Watch the sales representative's reaction to criticism of how he makes a sales pitch. Power? Notice who likes to influence decisions. Potential? Observe the sales representative as you tell him he's making the same mistakes he made when he started.

It should be obvious that profit, pride, power, participation and potential are things that all people seek from work. In addition, all of us want to be free of fear or, to put it another way, each of us wants to live in peace.

Six Motivational Needs Satisfied through Work:

- PRIDE
- POWER
- PARTICIPATION
- POTENTIAL
- PROFIT
- PEACE

Needs Vary, Ways Vary

The six motivational needs or motives are present in every person. They are in each of us almost from birth. The infant learns to fear the slap and learns to seek out the person that feeds and cares for him. That infant fear and infant love are the roots of the adult motivational needs.

Since no two infants are exposed to the same surroundings and the same people, the strength of these needs and the way the needs are satisfied vary. An example should make this clear.

Harry and Clark are both sales representatives. Both Harry and Clark have each of the six needs outlined above but the strength of these needs varies. Harry has a strong need to participate and Clark a weak need to participate. Both Harry and Clark have a strong need for pride. Harry satisfies his need for participation by being first in every contest. Clark satisfies his need for participation by being team safety chairman. Harry has a strong need for power and shows it by trying to control discussion meetings and in sales talks. Clark has a weaker need for control and usually tries to satisfy his need by playing the role of consultant to his retailers. Harry satisfies his need for pride by selling more products than anybody on the team. Clark satisfies his need for pride by keeping the best record books on the team.

As a manager, you must discover the strength of each of your sales representatives' needs and the way each of these needs is satisfied by the sales representatives who work for you. The easiest way to do this is to observe reactions and talk about each person. If you observe the reactions of a person to other people, to you and to different situations, you will begin to know each person. Discussing each person with your boss, with associates and with the person himself leads to greater knowledge. In this way, a *motivational profile* can be built on each sales representative. You can determine the strength of each need and how each need is satisfied. The practice exercise that follows has been developed to help you develop this skill.

PRACTICE EXERCISE: Motivational Profile

Choose a sales representative that you know well and complete the motivational profile presented below:

MOTIVATIONAL PROFILE   Name: _____

	Strength of Need			Way Satisfied
	Weak	Average	Strong	
PRIDE (Achievement, Recognition)				
POWER (Control, Dominate, Take Charge)				
PARTICIPATION (Affiliation, Social Approval)				
POTENTIAL (Grow, Develop)				
PROFIT (Dollar Motive)				
PEACE (Security)				

USING MOTIVES TO GET RESULTS

Motives can be used to get results by showing the people who work for you how they can satisfy their needs or motives in their jobs.

If the people who work for you have a *need to be proud,*

You should learn to:
- get each person involved
- show confidence in each person
- give credit and praise
- build pride in individual contributions

If the people who work for you have a *need for power,*

You should learn to:
- encourage their take charge attitudes
- reinforce dominant roles

If the people who work for you have a *need to participate,*

You should learn to:
- create a spirit of togetherness
- encourage each person to help others

If the people who work for you have a *need to fulfill potential,*

You should learn to:
- provide each person opportunities to become better.
- personally contribute to the development of each person and let them help you.

If the people who work for you have a *need to gain personal profit,*

You should learn to:
- get each person to tie-in dollars and work.
- use the possibility of a pay increase.

So much for the "dispenser of goodies." What about the "master of fear"? Obviously, we are proposing that the skillful use of fear is not only an effective motivator, but also a skill that can be built. We are in effect saying that peace, or absence of fear, is a need that can and should be used to get results. People will do things for you at work to keep or gain peace—the no-hassle state.

If the people who work for you have a *need to keep or gain peace,*

You should learn to:
* make productive use of fear

THE 14 MOTIVATIONAL COMMANDMENTS

As a manager, you can do the following things to encourage people to do what you want them to do:

1. Get each person involved
2. Show confidence in each person
3. Encourage the "take charge" attitudes
4. Reinforce the authoritative-consultant role
5. Give credit and praise to each person deserving it
6. Build pride in individual contributions
7. Create a spirit of togetherness
8. Encourage each person to help his fellow workers
9. Provide opportunities for each person to become better
10. Personally contribute to the development of each person and let them contribute to you
11. Get each person to tie-in dollars and work
12. Focus sales efforts by using commission incentives
13. Make productive use of fear
14. Assign blame and reprimand accordingly

These are the motivational skills a manager needs to have. These are the skills you need to develop if you do not currently possess them.

Get Each Person Involved

No matter what a person's work task is, that task will be performed better if the person is involved in it. If the work task is accepted as his responsibility, his part in the success of the business, it is done with personal commitment rather than with passing, peripheral interest. Getting things done, achieving things becomes increasingly important and personally satisfying.

Involvement can be built by a manager. Involvement requires a manager to recognize the ability of each person on the team to contribute to the success of the team. The profitable sale of the company's products is everybody's business, not just the manager's. Let your people know what profitable sales are and insist that they make them.

Every person who works for you can be encouraged to make a commitment to profitable sales. You must be willing to let your people question and make mistakes but remember the gamble is slight, you have pride working for you.

Get each person involved.

Show Confidence in Each Person

It is amazing how much can be accomplished if a manager only shows confidence in each person who works for him. Showing confidence really means that you trust each person to come through for you. While it is most likely that you have reservations about every sales representative who works for you, try to focus on what each can do. Give them a chance to prove to you what they can do. If you do not show confidence, they will never challenge themselves and consequently your reservations will increase rather than decrease.

The need to feel that others have confidence in you is universal. It really means that you trust them to do their job. Watching over them like a hawk damages their pride and limits what each person will do. We're speaking of the newest sales representative as well as the top sales representative on the team. Everyone has the need to be proud. By showing confidence, you let your people satisfy that need. "He trusts me, so I try to do it, I usually do," is the way one person put it.

Build confidence; use pride.

Encourage the "Take Charge" Attitude

As troublesome as the "take charge" attitude may be to your own desire to control and dominate, it is critical to the satisfaction of the power need of your salespeople. Encourage them to dominate and control all conversations with retailers involving buying decisions that affect their products.

Suggest a control-taking attitude.

Reinforce the Authoritative-Consultant Role

The best and safest way for a manager to see that his salespeople satisfy their need to control others without sacrificing sales is to reinforce the authoritative-consultant role. Pure power is offensive. Encouraging your salespeople to play the role of authoritative consultant allows them to satisfy their power needs without offending customers.

Build the consultant role.

Give Credit and Praise to Each Person Deserving It

Because a pat on the back and a simple word of compliment are easy to give, their immense motivational power can be overlooked. As you like to have your efforts praised, so also do your salespeople. A compliment to a sales representative for selling additional space in a key account appeals to his pride and makes him willing to do it again. Because each person has a need to be proud, the praise and credit you give is an effective motivator. If you are the "rewarder," you become a powerful force in directing team effort.

Some managers are a little self-conscious about giving out praise to older, more experienced salespeople. Like it or not, you are the father of the work family. If you don't praise, pride will not be satisfied.

Complimenting and praising is looked upon by some managers as a sign of weakness. "Everybody has his job to do—self-reward is good enough," they say. That's fine except recognition from the boss builds more pride than self-praise.

About the only time giving credit and praise isn't an effective motivator is when it is given and not deserved. When you give praise that has not been earned, the effectiveness of this powerful motivational tool is diminished.

Give credit and praise.

Build Pride in Individual Contributions

. Almost everyone does some things better than others. Try to find out what it is and let the person do it. For example: the sales representative with the knack for decorating can make the team meetings sparkle. Use this contribution which is uniquely his to build pride. Another example is the sales representative who likes math. Her contribution could be in setting contest goals. Still another is the minority sales representative who likes to recruit new sales representatives. Appeal to his pride and assign him the task of assisting you.

While this requires you to get to know your people as individuals, it pays off in a more productive work group and gives you the motivational tool you need.

Build pride.

Create a Spirit of Togetherness

Although each person has a need to be successful as an individual, he also has some need to participate in a group. Make each person feel like he is a part of the group.

The motivational power of togetherness is so strong that once developed you will immediately sense its effectiveness as a motivator. Togetherness can be built by treating your people as members of a team with you as the leader. Encourage your salespeople to get to know each other. Invite them to participate in solving problems that affect the team goals.

In effect you are building a team spirit. Each person will begin to do things for the good of the group. This sense of participation pays off and can be used to get people to do what you as the leader want them to do.

Use the team spirit.

Encourage Each Person to Help Other Team Members

Some managers overlook the power of participation and adopt the attitude: "Every person for himself." A much better attitude is:

"It's us against the team sales goals" or "If one of us doesn't do it, it won't get done." This is the interdependent attitude that can be built by a manager primarily because people really like to help other members of groups to which they belong.

Since there are plenty of examples of interdependence on most teams, this is not a new concept. One thing is quite clear though and that is that a great deal more use of this interdependence can be made.

Encourage interdependence.

Provide Opportunities for Each Person to Become Better

When a person first starts on a job, it's easy to help him become better. Providing opportunities for experienced people to become better is a little more difficult. Nonetheless, even the best can improve. A motivationally oriented manager looks for ways of helping even the most skillful and most experienced person to become better.

Conversations with the top sales representative about selling ideas you've used may be the way you help him. Asking the newest sales representative to assist you in developing the merchandising program may be the way to help him develop. There are all kinds of opportunities to help each person to become better. It's up to you to find them.

No one likes to do the same old job with the same level of skill all of their lives. Everyone wants to become better in some way, everyone wants to make the most of the potential they have.

Search for improvement opportunities.

Personally Contribute to Each Person and Let Him Contribute to You

A manager should be able to say, "There is something of me in each of them and something of each of them in me." This is about as clear a statement of the fulfillment of the potential need as can be made.

While it is probably clear how a manager can help each person grow, how can they help you grow? Listen, ask for suggestions and recognize the ideas that others have. As one sales representative put it, "New things happen every day. By sharing ideas, both of us can keep on learning."

Let them help you.

Get Each Person to Tie-In Dollars and Work

The power of the paycheck can easily be lost unless dollars paid and work done are tied together. Motivational skill consists of creating a relationship between pay and productivity. You are saying to the sales representative: Your efforts to sell merchandising ideas are directly contributing to the profitability of this team. Profitability is the reason companies stay in business. It's all too easy for a sales representative to forget that the work he does contributes to the success or failure of the company.

Remind each person that paychecks and productivity go together.

Focus Sales Efforts by Using the Commission Incentive

We know from our own experience that the possibility of making commission motivates people. The following comment to a sales representative by a manager is perhaps a good example of this: "Look, you want more money, we need more sales. I'll trade you—more sales for more commission dollars." Commission incentives can be used to focus sales efforts.

Use commission incentives to focus activity.

Make Productive Use of Fear

Whether we like to admit it or not, people do things when they are afraid. Although McGregor and other psychologists suggest that fear is overused in the business world, the truth may well be that it is poorly used rather than overused. A threat of firing, when a strong union makes this impossible, is a good example of poor use of fear. Using fear excessively or exclusively leads to terror and while fear moves, terror immobilizes. Consequently learning to make productive use of fear requires you as a manager to determine how much fear to use and how you can constructively threaten each person who works for you.

There is a big difference between making the statement that work reports must be turned in on time, and telling the person that he'll be fired if he's even one second late. The first is likely to be an effective use of fear, the second is overuse.

Many new managers are at first repelled at the thought that they must use fear. They soon marvel at how effective it is when all else fails. That is usually when overuse sets in. Peace becomes impossible and fear becomes ineffective.

Don't fear fear, use it wisely.

Assign Blame and Reprimand Accordingly

When things go wrong, someone is at fault. At times it is readily apparent who "goofed" and it's easy to assign blame. At other times, determining who is at fault is more difficult. It's up to you to assign blame and if appropriate, punish the negligent person. People expect to be blamed if they err and are willing to accept penalties when they do err.

Let's say that you find the sales reports are consistently not being properly completed by one of your sales representatives. It's up to you to assign blame. A verbal reprimand is probably in order.

The motivational role we are proposing is not the all knowing judge and punitive jailer, it is simply the role of functioning leader. As one manager put it, "If you want peace around here, don't goof."

Blame and reprimand.

Each of these motivational skills can be built with effort and practice. Evaluate your skill level in using each of the motivational forces. If you find yourself weak in an area concentrate on building skill in that area.

SO WHAT'S NEW?

The matter of motivation is not new. Every manager, every leader motivates. Everyone has some skill in using each of these six forces within man to get others to do what he wants them to do. The big problem is in using all six forces. Peace and profit are only two of the forces and threatening and offering incentives only two of the motivational approaches. All too frequently in times of stress and frustration, pride and giving credit, power and customer control, participation and using team spirit, potential and helping others develop are just plain forgotten. When they are, the manager is functioning on two-sixths of his motivational power. So what's new? There are six forces and six motivational approaches. Learn to use all six.

A Brief Review

So far we have been talking about motivational needs, have suggested ways of using these needs to motivate workers and have pointed out that the strength of needs vary and have indicated that needs can be satisfied in various ways. Now it's time to talk about the motivational process.

IT DEPENDS ON HOW YOU PUT IT

Almost anything you want a person to do, he will do if you put it to him in the right way. People can be motivated to do almost anything—from keeping records to selling special floor displays—if you state what you want them to do in terms that will appeal to their individual motivational makeup. The process of motivating an individual to do something looks like this:

Motivational Process

1. Know the individual.
2. Know specifically what you want the person to do.
3. Determine how he sees what you want him to do.
4. State what you want the person to do in terms that will appeal to his motivational makeup and be consistent with his view.

Let's take an example:

Sales representative Don never follows the call schedule. The system requires him to do it but he doesn't. He seems to feel that making calls on schedule is depriving him of his individuality. You've pointed out the additional sales he is missing but that doesn't seem to work.

The motivational question is how to get Don to make calls on schedule. The two motivational forces that worked were: pride and participation. The manager used this approach, "You are the most experienced, the other sales representatives follow your example and as a result call schedules are not being followed. As a result our shelf and floor display goals are not being reached. Will you set the example and make calls on schedule?" Simple, but it worked.

MORE ON THE MOTIVATIONAL PROCESS

Since the motivational process begins with a knowledge of the person you are trying to motivate, get to know each person who works for you as an individual. Although you may know exactly what you want a person to do, it's not always clear to the person you are trying to motivate. Take time to define clearly in your own mind what it is you want done before you try to motivate someone to do it. Determining how the person you are trying to motivate sees or perceives what you want him to do is important primarily because his view may interfere with what you want him to do. If for example, a person sees what you want him to do "somebody else's job" or "too much to ask," you have to deal with that perception. Stating what you want done is basically a communication skill.

In our example, sales representative Don just wouldn't make calls on schedule until his interest in team sales and his pride in being the example was tied in with what you wanted him to do— make calls on schedule. While the motivational process requires you to think before you speak, it will pay off, primarily because motivation has a great deal to do with "how you put it."

PRACTICE EXERCISE: Using the Motivational Process

Using the following information, decide on a motivational approach to get George Bronson to do what you think he should be doing.

Background Information:

- Mr. Bronson is 38 years old, married and has three children.
- He has two years of college but no degree.
- His interests outside work include gardening and scouting.
- He owns a medium sized apartment complex worth about $100,000.

Work Record:

- Prior work experience includes 8 years as a clerk and store manager in one of the large chains.
- He has been working for you about two years and is currently making about $18,000 a year which includes commission every month.

How others describe him:

- A quiet guy but once you draw him out, he really knows how to talk.
- When scared, he moves.
- Not very ambitious—he's got what he wants.
- A good implementer but a poor planner.
- Competitive, if you can reach him.

Current motivational problem:

- He is the type of person who holds on to business but is not good at building sales. Sales on all of the other routes have grown but sales on his route have kept steady—loosing some here and gaining some there.
- Most of the store people like him and he likes them but there are a few head clerks that he can't get along with.
- Mr. Bronson doesn't like to sell—he feels he can get more done if he doesn't make a big thing out of asking for things. He uses the slide-in approach.

1. Describe George Bronson's *motivational makeup*.

_____

_____

2. *State clearly what* you want him to do that he is not doing.

_____

_____

3. How do you think Bronson *perceives* what you want him to do?

_____

_____

4. State what you want him to do in terms that will appeal to his motivational makeup and be consistent with his perception of what you want him to do.

_____

_____

SUMMARY: MOTIVATE EACH PERSON WHO WORKS FOR YOU

While our opening paragraph stated our message quite clearly —A manager motivates by becoming a master of fear and a dispenser of goodies—some elaboration on this message has been made.

Motivation was defined as the things a manager can do to get people to do what he wants them to do. A motive was defined as a force within a person that can be used to move him.

The *six motivational needs* of every person are: pride, power, participation, potential, profit and peace. Each of these needs varies in strength and the way the need is satisfied varies.

Fourteen motivational commandments were listed. They are: Get each person involved. Show confidence in each person. Give credit and praise to each person deserving it. Encourage the take-charge attitude. Reinforce the authoritative-consultant role. Build pride in individual contributions. Create a spirit of togetherness. Encourage each person to help his fellow workers. Provide opportunities for each person to become better. Personally contribute to the development of each person and let them help you. Get each person to tie in dollars and work. Stimulate activity by using the possibility of a pay increase. Make productive use of fear. Assign blame and reprimand accordingly.

A *four-step motivational process* was outlined: Know the individual, define clearly what you want him to do, find out how he sees what you want him to do, state clearly what you want him to do in terms that will appeal to his motivational makeup and be consistent with how he sees what you want him to do.

QUESTIONS THAT NEED ANSWERS

To be sure that you understand the ideas discussed in this section, answer the following questions.

1. Motivation has to do with the way a manager:
    a) handles and pays people.
    b) gives orders and resolves grievances.
    c) manipulates people.
    d) gets people to do what he wants them to do.

2. Which of the following is not one of the motivational needs listed:
    a) peace.
    b) profit.
    c) pain.
    d) participation.

3. The strength of each of the motivational needs:
    a) is the same.
    b) is based on an experience.
    c) varies.
    d) remains constant.

4. If the people that work for you have a need to be proud, you should:
    a) create a spirit of togetherness.
    b) get each person involved.
    c) contribute to their development.
    d) use the possibility of a pay increase.

5. Which of the following is a motivational commandment:
    a) make productive use of fear.
    b) build pride in individual contributions.
    c) assign blame and reprimand accordingly.
    d) all of these.

6. Which of the motivational commandments is violated by watching over a sales representative like a hawk:
   a) personally contribute to each.
   b) create a spirit of togetherness.
   c) build pride in individual contributions.
   d) show confidence in each.

7. Interdependence is the result of the salesperson's need for:
   a) pride.
   b) participation.
   c) profit.
   d) peace.

8. Motivationally speaking, a paycheck:
   a) has no meaning.
   b) appeals to the profit need.
   c) appeals to the unemployed.
   d) is a good club.

9. The statement, "It depends on how you put it" refers to how you:
   a) state what you want done.
   b) modify the message.
   c) suggest what you want done.

10. Motivating a person to do something begins with:
    a) knowing how to state it.
    b) knowing the results desired.
    c) knowing yourself.
    d) knowing the person.

If you made the following choices, you should feel that the ideas discussed are yours: 1d, 2c, 3c, 4b, 5d, 6d, 7b, 8b, 9a, 10d.

Chapter 4

Recruiting and Selecting Salespeople

THE TELEPHONE RINGS

The telephone rings. Your most promising sales representative informs you that she is resigning in two weeks. Because she had been doing so well, you are caught by surprise. After efforts to convince her to stay fail, the reality hits you—you need to find a new sales representative within two weeks or you'll have to cover the territory yourself.

It would be great if you had a farm team to call on for replacements, but most sales organizations don't afford you such a luxury. You must find a qualified person outside your organization and find that person fast. You must recruit and select a sales applicant.

This chapter is all about finding and selecting salespeople. The selection you make will determine your effectiveness in the sales territory being vacated. Anyone can hire a replacement; it takes special skill to recruit and select an effective salesperson.

Three questions will be asked and answered in this chapter. The questions are: What kind of person makes the best salesperson for your team? Where can this kind of person be found? How can you determine whether an applicant really has what it takes to be a productive member of your team? The topics discussed in this chapter are: developing job specifications, recruiting qualified applicants, evaluating applicants, and making an informed selection decision.

KNOW THE SPECIFICATIONS BEFORE YOU START LOOKING

Although this seems obvious, many field sales managers are so busy running a sales team that they never take the time to think about the kind of person they really want working for them.

In thinking about hiring a salesperson, there are three things that you should know. These are: 1) the knowledge required to do the job; 2) the skills required to do the job; and 3) the personal qualities necessary for the job. The process of thinking through job specifications is called job analysis.

The job specifications for a consumer product package goods sales representative might include the following:

1. Skill in doing basic arithmetic and keeping records.
2. Knowledge of in-store merchandising.
3. Familiarity with chain-store operations.
4. Basic selling skills—get attention, tell a sales story, overcome objections and close.
5. Familiarity with geographical territory.
6. Skill in dealing with people.
7. Management potential.
8. Command presence.
9. Smart yet practical.
10. Drive and energy.

By thinking through the knowledge, skills and personal qualities needed to do the job before you start considering applicants, you are much less likely to be influenced by the pressures of the moment. While the job specifications are seldom ever completely met, they give you a criterion for evaluating objectively each applicant you consider.

PRACTICE EXERCISE: Job Analysis

Answer the three following questions about the sales representatives on your team.

Question 1: What knowledge is required?

_____

_____

_____

_____

Question 2: What technical or sales skills are required to do this job?

_____

_____

_____

_____

Question 3: What personal qualities are necessary to do this job (work, approach, thinking, with others, emotional)?

_____

_____

_____

_____

FINDING PEOPLE: RECRUITING

Qualified people don't usually walk through the door when you need them. This is true even in times when jobs are hard to find. Some qualified people do walk in and ask for jobs, but this is the exception rather than the rule. If qualified people don't come to you, then you must seek them out. In looking for qualified people, you should make use of many sources: referrals, employment agencies, newspaper ads, and school placement offices.

Sources of Qualified People:
- Referrals
- Agencies
- Newspaper ads
- School placement offices
- Walk-ins

Referrals

Present employees and business associates are a good source of new salespeople. Referrals can be used to find experienced salespeople working for competitors or qualified but inexperienced applicants who are ready to be trained. Encourage your people and friends to refer others to you who they think will make good salespeople for your sales team.

Suggested guidelines for the use of referrals to recruit are:

1) Make it clear what you are looking for in terms of job requirements and personal qualifications.

2) Always thank the person who makes referrals whether or not you hire the person referred.

Employment Agencies

Both state and private employment agencies can help you find qualified people. The only requirement is that you make clear the knowledge, skill and personal qualities you are looking for.

Guidelines for use of agencies to recruit include the following:

1) Work with one particular person in each agency. This way your company and sales job will be familiar to that person.

2) Clearly specify the job you want to fill and the qualities and degree of experience you want in an applicant.

3) Restrict the number of people you will see. Specifying only three to five referrals from the agency will encourage agency screening.

4) Be sure the question of agency fee is agreed on prior to seeing applicants.

Newspaper Ads

Newspaper ads are particularly effective when you are trying to find experienced people. If you select a paper with good circulation, you are likely to get a large number of applicants. This will give you an opportunity to select the very best possible candidates from a large pool. While some of the applicants will not be qualified, many will be worth interviewing.

In order for an ad to be effective, it must be carefully written with whatever details are necessary. Let's examine an ad that appeared recently in a major newspaper.

FOOD SALES CAREER

National Foods Inc., a multi-million dollar Food Corp., is expanding and needs sales representatives to work in the S.I. area.

WE OFFER

1. Complete training program with pay.
2. Qualified appointments.
3. Many company benefits.

For appt. call Ms. Rogers, 835-1500 Ext. 200

This ad includes: 1) the name of the company, which attracts attention, 2) the location of territory that is available, 3) why the opening exists, 4) the sense of immediate need in the invitation to apply by telephone.

The ad, however, has several deficiencies. Among them: 1) the rate of pay is not mentioned, 2) the type of sales job is not clear, 3) the preferred time to call is omitted.

Now let's look at the following two ads:

SALES REPRESENTATIVE

Experienced headquarter sales represent-ative wanted by national grocery prod-ucts company. Our salespeople are proud to work for us and say "we get paid for sales results." If you think you are good enough, send a resume to: _____

FOOD CHAIN
SALES REPRESENTATIVE

Sales representative currently calling on food chain headquarters for a national grocery company. Must know local chains and have merchandising expertise. Base pay: 18 plus car, expenses and commis-sion. Send resume to: _____ or call _____ for a confidential telephone interview.

The ad at the top headlines the broad job, "Sales Representa-tive," the ad at the bottom: "Food Chain Sales Representative." Since the job is for an experienced salesperson, the second title is better. The first ad talks in generalities about pay and benefits. The second ad is specific. The ad at the bottom specifies the required knowledge and experience: floor and shelf merchandising knowledge and chain headquarter experience.

Keep in mind that like most ads, these are small and hard to read. The most important idea in writing an ad, therefore, is to attract as well as screen applicants. If there are any special features that the job has, they should be stated as requirements rather than as mere preferences.

The final statement of your ad should indicate how you want the applicants to reply: by letter or by telephone. While asking applicants to write in is the most convenient method for you, more applicants will reply if they are given an opportunity to call.

An effective way of handling telephone call-ins is to have a secretary answer the calls and record the following basic information:

RECORD OF TELEPHONE APPLICANTS
WHO ANSWER NEWSPAPER AD

DATE OF AD _____

NAME _____ PHONE # _____

ADDRESS _____ AREA CODE _____

HIGH SCHOOL GRADUATE _____ DATE _____

EXTENT OF COLLEGE TRAINING: _____

CURRENT POSITION _____
_____

HOW LONG THERE _____ CURRENT SALARY _____

PRIOR POSITION #1 _____
_____

HOW LONG THERE _____ SALARY _____

SALARY REQUIREMENTS _____

WHEN AVAILABLE _____

WOULD YOU BE WILLING TO RELOCATE AFTER ONE YEAR _____
_____

This information will allow you to screen the applicants and call back the most qualified first.

Another question that should be discussed is whether you identify the company or use a blind ad. Generally ads which identify the company get more replies than blind ads. The only disadvantage of identifying your company is that you are under some obligation to send a reply to those that apply. A blind ad makes this a less pressing obligation.

In summary, guidelines for use of newspaper ads to recruit should include the following:

1. Write the ad so that it attracts as well as screens candidates.

2. Use a blind ad with a box number if you don't want to identify yourself.

3. Use an ad with a telephone number if you want to get applicants quickly.

School Placement Offices

School placement offices are an excellent source of salespeople if you are prepared to train them. While most graduates have limited experience, there are those who have sold on a part-time basis and would welcome a career in selling.

Placement officers are usually very cooperative if you give them the necessary information about your sales job and your specifications.

Suggested guidelines to follow in using placement offices to recruit are:

1. Call the school placement offices and tell them what your needs are.

2. Visit the school and get to know the people in the placement office. This will usually open the lines of communication and will often render you a little extra personal attention.

Walk-Ins

Since many people who walk into your office looking for a sales job are not really qualified, there is a danger of overlooking even qualified people. To make productive use of walk-ins, you need an efficient system for separating the qualified from the unqualified. Such a system is outlined on the next page:

1. Each walk-in is given an application form to complete in the office. No interviews are given that day.

2. Screen the application forms and schedule a preliminary interview for those that are qualified.

3. Send a letter to all walk-in applicants who complete the form and thank them for their interest in your company.

The following chart summarizes the advantages and disadvantages of each recruiting source that has been discussed.

Advantages	Disadvantages
Referrals	
• Applicants are known by the person referring them.	• Turning applicants down can be a bit difficult and awkward.
Employment Agencies	
• Applicants you interview have already been prescreened.	• Applicants are not always available immediately.
Newspaper Ads	
• Large number of applicants, quickly. • Low cost for getting applicants.	• Many unqualified people must be screened out.
School Placement	
• People often have growth potential.	• Applicants are usually inexperienced. • Many applicants are just shopping.
Walk-Ins	
• Constant source of available applicants. • No cost for getting applicants.	• Many unqualified people must be screened out.

Recruiting Roster

A vacant territory means lost sales. Since it often takes time to find the right person, it is a good idea to maintain an up-to-date roster or file of promising candidates to fill any open territory should a vacancy occur. Some sales managers keep a recruiting roster so that they can record the names and contact information of qualified candidates they find when they have no vacancies.

NEEDED: INFORMATION TO MAKE A SELECTION DECISION

Whether you are choosing one of two available applicants for a vacant territory, or one of the five applicants to replace your top sales producer who is retiring in three weeks, you are making a selection decision. In order to make a good decision, you need certain kinds of information. This information can be obtained in several ways. You can look for information on application forms. You can conduct interviews. You can check business and personal references. And you can give tests. Since each source provides some information not available from the others, all four sources should be used.

How to Select the Best Person:
- Application forms
- Interviews
- References
- Tests

WHY APPLICATION FORMS?

To most job applicants, application forms are a necessary evil and to most field sales managers, just more paper. But a good application form can give you vital information, can eliminate unqualified people from your consideration, and can reduce the time you spend interviewing. A good deal of basic information such as address, job history, and education can be obtained more quickly and efficiently through an application form than in an interview.

A good application form can quickly eliminate many candidates on the basis of inexperience or lack of skill. To be effective, an application form must ask questions that will give you information you need to make your selection decision. It should be a form that can be completed relatively quickly and easily by the applicant, and evaluated quickly by the manager to determine the information he needs. Ease of completion, ease of evaluation and effectiveness of questions in getting the right information are the three things that should be kept in mind in developing or choosing an application form for sales applicants.

Familiarize Yourself with the Application Form

In most instances you are not free to choose the application form that will be used. You can, however, familiarize yourself with the application form furnished by your company and know where to look on the application form for the information you need. You should know where to look for information on the applicant's skills or special knowledge. You should know where you can look to determine whether the applicant is a worker or a drifter. Taking the time to familiarize yourself with the application form makes it much easier to use as a source of information and as a screening tool.

PRACTICE EXERCISE: Screening an Application Form

In order to build your skills in screening application forms, study the application form completed by Ralph Barron, which is presented on the following pages. Then answer the questions on the basis of his responses.

List five facts you know about Ralph Barron from reading the application form. Consider his knowledge, skills and personal qualities.

_____

_____

_____

List three questions that you would ask Ralph in the interview.

_____

_____

_____

Based on the information presented on the application form, would you hire Ralph Barron for the job he's applying for? Give reasons.

_____

_____

_____

JOB APPLICATION FORM

PERSONAL DATA

Name (print) **BARRON, RALPH**   Soc. Sec. No. _____   Date **10/8/69**
Last   First   Middle

Present address **510 DIAMOND ST.   L.A.   CALIF.**   Home Tel. No. **213   487-1410**
No.   Street   City   State   Zip   Area Code   Number

Previous address _____   Dates resided there: _____
No.   Street   City   State   Zip   From   to

Weight **180**   Height **6'1"**   Are You A U.S. Citizen? ☐ Yes ☐ No   If No, Are You A Permanent Resident? ☐ Yes ☐ No

Have you ever Been Refused Bond?   ☐ Yes ☒ No   } If Yes to Either, _____

Have You Been Convicted of a   ☐ Yes ☒ No   } Explain.   _____
Crime Other Than Minor Traffic Violations?

Do you have full use of a car for your work? **YES**   What type of license do you have? **DRIVERS**

Make, model and year of car(s) owned _____   Driver's License # **A-265531**

Was your operator's permit ever suspended? _____ No_____ Yes; Auto Accidents: Date(s) _____

If yes, why? _____

Auto Insurance: Collision $ _____   Liability $ _____

EDUCATION

SCHOOL—LOCATION	MAJOR	YRS. OF ATTENDANCE From	To	DEGREE	GRADUATION Date-Mo./Year	GRADE POINT Avg./Out of
HIGH SCHOOL **DALLAS, TEXAS**	**MATH HISTORY**					
VOCATIONAL OR TRADE SCHOOL						
COLLEGE **TEXAS STATE**	**L. ARTS**		**6/67**	**B.A.**	**6/67**	**3.1 / 4**
☐ COLLEGE or ☐ GRADUATE SCHOOL						
OTHER SPECIAL SKILLS AND/OR TRAINING						

Subjects liked best **MATH, HISTORY, HUMANITIES, PSYCHOLOGY**   Subjects liked least **SCIENCE, ECONOMICS**

Proportion of expenses earned in high school **25%**   In college **100%**

PHYSICAL

Weight **180**   Height **6'1"**   Build **SLIM**   Condition of health **GOOD**

List illnesses, operations, accidents (with dates) **FLU, '66**

Any form of nervousness **No**   stomach trouble **No**   allergies **HAY FEVER**

back pain **No**   headaches **No**   sleeping habits **GOOD**

POSITION

Position Desired **SALESMAN**   Salary Expected **$7500.00**

Referred to us by? **NEWSPAPER AD**   Date Available **AS SOON AS THERE IS AN OPENING**

Are You Willing to Travel ☐ Never ☐ 25% of Time ☐ 50% of Time ☐ Over 50% of Time?

Are You Willing to Relocate? **X** Yes _____ No

GOALS: What kind of work do you most like **SALES NOW, SALES MANAGEMENT LATER**

Salary you expect — Next year **$8500.00**   In five years **$15,000.00**

What are your plans for the future? **SALES MANAGEMENT CAREER. PROVIDE A GOOD STANDARD OF LIVING FOR MY FUTURE FAMILY.**

NAME OF MOST RECENT EMPLOYER ACE CANDY.	YOUR TITLE SALESMAN	EMPLOYED FROM 7/67 TO PRESENT	SALARY $575 START END PER MO.
STREET ADDRESS 100 ALMER		REASON FOR SEEKING CHANGE TOO CLOSE SUPERVISION + LIMITED GROWTH OPPORTUNITY FOR MANAGEMENT	
CITY LOS ANGELES, STATE CALIF. ZIP CODE		PERSON REPORTED TO BOB CAMPBELL	
TYPE OF BUSINESS: PRODUCER OF CANDY		POSITION SALES MANAGER	PHONE & EXT.
MAY WE CONTACT? Yes ☒ No ☐			
DESCRIPTION OF YOUR DUTIES SELLING AND SERVICING OF ACE DISTRIBUTORS.			

E M P L O Y M E N T   H I S T O R Y

NAME OF EMPLOYER CITY OF DALLAS	YOUR TITLE YOUTH CAMP LEADER	EMPLOYED FROM 66 TO 67	SALARY $300 START END MO.
STREET ADDRESS		REASON FOR SEEKING CHANGE SUMMERS ONLY	
CITY DALLAS STATE TEXAS ZIP CODE		PERSON REPORTED TO HAL WILLIAMS	
TYPE OF BUSINESS: CITY GOVERNMENT		POSITION	PHONE & EXT.
MAY WE CONTACT? Yes ☒ No ☐			
DESCRIPTION OF YOUR DUTIES DIRECTION AND SUPERVISION OF CAMP ACTIVITIES.			

NAME OF EMPLOYER FRANK'S STATIONERY	YOUR TITLE SALES CLERK	EMPLOYED FROM 63 TO 66	SALARY START END
STREET ADDRESS		REASON FOR SEEKING CHANGE PART TIME	
CITY STATE ZIP CODE		PERSON REPORTED TO	
TYPE OF BUSINESS:		POSITION	PHONE & EXT.
MAY WE CONTACT? Yes ☐ No ☐			
DESCRIPTION OF YOUR DUTIES SELL STATIONERY SUPPLIES			

NAME OF EMPLOYER	YOUR TITLE	EMPLOYED FROM TO	SALARY START END
STREET ADDRESS		REASON FOR SEEKING CHANGE	
CITY STATE ZIP CODE		PERSON REPORTED TO	
TYPE OF BUSINESS:		POSITION	PHONE & EXT.
MAY WE CONTACT? Yes ☐ No ☐			
DESCRIPTION OF YOUR DUTIES			

C E R T I F I C A T I O N

SIGNATURE Ralph Barron	DATE

INTERVIEWING APPLICANTS

The purpose of the interview is to give you an opportunity to tell the applicant about your sales job and to give the applicant an opportunity to tell you something about himself and his abilities.

An interview has aptly been defined as "a conversation between two scared people who would both rather be doing something else." The manager, who would rather be managing than interviewing, is scared he'll miss some important information that will later haunt him. The applicant, who knows he's being judged by what he says, is scared he'll say the wrong thing.

You don't have to be a personnel specialist or a clinical psychologist in order to conduct a timely, fact-finding interview. The basic interview skill required is the ability to carry on a conversation with another person. It means listening carefully and asking intelligent questions. This is something you do every day. In all conversations, you are trying to find out what another person thinks. That is not too much different from getting information from an applicant. What is different is that you are less familiar with an interviewee than you are with an acquaintance.

As in any conversation the questions that are asked influence the facts that are offered. The information you give to the applicant and the way you give it will determine his interest in and reaction to the job. An interview is simply a conversation in which questions are asked and information exchanged.

THE QUICK, FACT-FINDING, INTEREST-BUILDING INTERVIEW

While every interview is personal and unique, you can learn how to conduct a quick, fact-finding conversation with each applicant. Here are some important suggestions.

How to Conduct Fact-Finding Interviews:

1. Talk in private.
2. Ask open-ended questions to get the applicant talking.
3. Ask questions about specifications.
4. Don't ask questions already answered on the application form.
5. Use test questions to validate skills and knowledge.
6. Encourage the applicant to talk about past employment.
7. Record your observations on paper.
8. Make sure the applicant understands the job.
9. Tell the applicant what happens next. Hire or hold.

Talk in Private

Thirty minutes of uninterrupted conversation will give you the information you need to make most hiring decisions. A sixty-minute conversation with many interruptions will stop your train of thought and will hinder the conversation. This is frustrating to both you and the interviewee. You will probably be left with less information. The interviewee will get the impression that your interruptions are more important than he is. This is rude as well as inconsiderate conduct. As one applicant put it, "I was asked to be here at 10:30 and then I was kept waiting fifteen minutes. Almost as soon as the interview started, the telephone rang and it kept on ringing. By the time he was off the phone, I was so annoyed, I didn't want the job anymore."

Interruptions can be prevented if you insist on private interviews. If you interview in an office, insist that your salespeople not interrupt you. If you interview in the field, choose a place where you cannot be interrupted; a private booth in a coffee shop, a hotel room are examples of places where private interviews can be conducted.

Ask Open-Ended Questions

Open-ended questions are those that can't be answered by a simple "yes" or "no." They are "how," "why" or "what" questions—questions that require thoughtful and sometimes lengthy explanations. When you interview, you should always try to phrase your questions in an open-ended way so that the interviewee can expand and amplify what is said. This will give the interviewee a chance to show what he knows and how he thinks, and will allow you the chance to get to know him better. For example, rather than asking something like, "Do you like your current job?", you might ask, "What do you like or dislike most about your current job?" This is also likely to give you more information than a closed question. Some other open-ended questions might also be: "What have you done in the past that you're proud of?", "What experience have you had that will help you do this job?", "Why did you leave that job?"

Ask Questions about Specifications

Let's say, the specifications for the sales job are:

- Skill in expressing ideas
- Knowledge of merchandising
- Skill in influencing others
- Management potential

The following questions are examples of ones that will help get the information needed about the applicant's qualifications for the job: *Skill in expressing ideas:* Tell me about yourself. Why did you choose your major in school? Do you think salespeople are born or made? *Skill in influencing others:* What is the most difficult sale you have ever made? What would you do if you walked into a store and the retailer told you to get out? What should be included in every sales presentation? *Knowledge of merchandising:* What would you tell a new sales representative about in-store merchandising if you were the manager? What do you think about the way Campbell's soups are shelved in supermarkets? What is the best merchandised store you have ever been in? *Management potential:* What leadership positions have you had in the past? What suggestions would you give a manager for supervising salespeople? The answers the applicant gives to these questions will help you determine if he or she meets the specifications for the job.

Don't Ask Questions Already Answered on the Application Form

Midway through the interview the applicant looks you square in the eye and says, "You're asking me questions I already answered on the application form." While some of the information on the application form needs to be verified and expanded, such basic questions as "Are you working now?" should not be asked if it has already been answered on the application form. To save time and to show that you have carefully reviewed the application and are familiar with the applicant's qualifications, don't ask questions that can be found by reading the application form.

Use Test Questions to Validate Skills and Knowledge

Test questions help to eliminate the person who claims to have skills and knowledge that he does not have. Some kind of test question should always be asked. For example, if you ask an experienced salesperson to explain how to overcome an objection, he should be able to answer you. If he doesn't understand the question, you have probably spotted a phony. Again, a sales applicant who cannot answer questions about merchandising may not have the experience claimed. So try to have one or two test questions to validate the skill and knowledge needed for each job.

Encourage the Applicant to Talk about the Past

Information about how a person handled past jobs is more reliable than hypothetical information about what he might do in future situations. This is particularly important when you are trying to evaluate personal qualities. For example, asking a question like, "Why do you think you were successful?" gives more meaningful information than the question, "Why do you think you will be successful in this job if you get it?" The first question encourages factual answers based on real situations; the second question encourages fantasy answers. Of course, if a person acted incorrectly the first time and learned from the experience, this is also an important fact to keep in mind.

Record Your Observations on Paper

Remembering all of the information you obtain from an interview is difficult unless you write it down on paper. Some managers use the application form; others use scrap paper; and still others develop their own interview comments forms. The interview comments form lists the knowledge, skills and personal qualities required of a particular job on the left side of the paper. The right side of the form is used to record comments. The following interview comments form was used to interview applicants for entry level sales jobs.

The interview comments form helps you remember the applicant's qualities that you gathered from your conversation. It also helps you to organize and structure your thoughts more quickly and concisely.

INTERVIEW COMMENTS
SALES APPLICANTS

Applicant: _____ Address: _____

Considered For: _____ Referred By: _____

Interviewed By: _____ Date: _____

The following interview check list pertains to applicant listed above. Comments regarding applicant's general qualifications for other positions should be listed under "Remarks."

	Poor	Average	Above Average	Superior	Comments
Skill in expressing ideas					
Drive—energy					
Command presence					
Skill in dealing with people					
Ability to learn					
Interest in job					
Selling ability					
Management potential					
Awareness of merchandising principles					
Job stability					
OVERALL RATING					

Remarks:

_____

_____

Recommendations:

Hire: _____ Hold: _____ Reject: _____

Make Sure the Applicant Understands the Job

"This is not the job I was hired to do." Hearing this comment from a new employee is not a unique experience. While some applicants tend not to hear the difficult or tedious parts of the job when you explain them many managers fail to mention them. If you hire someone for a rural territory and forget to tell them that the job entails three nights a week overnight travel, you shouldn't be surprised if the person leaves. After several experiences like this, you'll soon see why it's important that the applicant understands the job completely before accepting it. So tell it the way it is: the good and the bad, the easy and the hard, the glamorous and the gloomy.

Tell the Applicant What Happens Next

You conversation with the applicant should lead to some goal. You should conclude by either offering the applicant the job on the spot, asking the person to call after you've seen all of the applicants, or putting him in a "hold" file. Putting an applicant on "hold" means telling him that nothing is available now, but when it is, you will call. Since all job offers are preceded by reference checks, test results, and physical examination, be sure to mention that your offer is subject to positive information from these sources.

PITFALLS TO AVOID

While interviewing is a skill you can build, being aware of common pitfalls will help you be more effective. Here are some rules you might want to remember and follow.

1. Avoid Personal Bias

As a manager, you should make decisions about the applicant on the basis of qualifications. Hiring or disqualifying a candidate because of some personal mannerism or physical characteristic that has nothing to do with the job is both unprofessional and unwise.

Some managers make their decisions on the basis of one specific trait—dress, forcefulness, etc., thus judging the applicant's total worth by that one trait alone. This is referred to as the "halo effect."

"Hire that person. She is a sharp dresser," might be the kind of comment such a manager would make. Listen carefully and try wherever possible to judge the applicant on his or her ability to sell rather than on other external and insignificant facts.

2. Avoid Super-Selling

Sometimes in interviewing, a manager will try to sell the job to the applicant rather than letting the applicant sell himself. This kind of manager often fails to get the right kind of information to insure a good match. He can also turn off qualified applicants who are suspicious of his anxiousness to make the job seem pleasing. These applicants feel there must be something wrong with a job that a manager has to push so hard.

3. Don't Out-Talk the Applicant

Some managers who are nervous when they first interview talk to cover up their anxiousness. Others simply enjoy listening to the sound of their own voices. When this occurs, the manager learns very little about the applicant.

In interviewing, try to remember to let the applicant speak as much as possible. One sign of a good interviewer is his or her ability to encourage and bring out an applicant. By encouraging applicants to say what they think and how they feel, you can learn a great deal about them and their qualifications.

PRACTICE EXERCISE: Interpreting Answers to Interview Questions

Getting answers is one thing. Interpreting them is another.

Five questions that were actually asked in an interview and the answers that were given are presented below. What would you conclude about the person from the answers given? Write your conclusions on the lines below.

Question 1: Tell me about yourself.
Answer: There's not much to tell. I was born here, raised here and I'll probably die here.
From the response, the interviewee would seem to be _____

_____

Question 2: Do you ever lose your temper?
Answer: Hell no!
From the response, the interviewee would seem to be _____

_____

Question 3: Why do you want this job?
Answer: Well, I like to eat. And besides, I can do the job with one hand tied behind my back.
From the response, the interviewee would seem to be _____

_____

Question 4: Are you a steady worker?
Answer: I sure am. I haven't missed a day's work in a year. I'd still be working at my old job if we hadn't gotten a new house out here.
From the response, the interviewee would seem to be _____

_____

Question 5: Can you start tomorrow?
Answer: I'll need to give notice where I'm working now. Can I start a week from tomorrow?
From the response, the interviewee would seem to be _____

_____

CHECKING REFERENCES

The information you get from the application form and from the interview gives you a good indication of the applicant's abilities and qualifications. However, these sources tell you nothing about an applicant's *work reputation*. One of the most effective ways of determining this is through reference checking.

Reference checking can give you an idea of how other people view the applicant and his work on a daily basis over a period of time. While most employers don't like to speak badly of a former employee, they are willing to verify dates of employment, to indicate any major problems in the person's performance, and to give you a general idea of work habits and reputation.

Generally, the best approach in checking references is to get factual information first. For example, the dates of employment and the nature of his work. Then, a more personal question like, "What was his reputation as a worker in your company?" or "What were the reasons he gave for leaving?" can be asked.

All information obtained from telephone reference checking should be checked from all points of view. A negative reference must be viewed in terms of the job the person was performing. For example, a report that a sales applicant was too restless for clerical work is a negative but it should be expected from a person who will be successful in sales.

TEST RESULTS

One additional source of information on applicants comes from tests. This includes both technical tests that evaluate an applicant's product knowledge, and psychological tests that measure the applicant's personal qualities.

While selection decisions for most consumer product package goods sales positions do not require an evaluation of technical knowledge, whenever they do, a written test should be given to determine technical competency. Technical knowledge is most efficiently and accurately evaluated through the use of written tests.

The use of psychological tests to evaluate personality characteristics is a much more involved question. Psychological tests which measure personality traits or personal qualities have come under a great deal of fire in the past decade. Minority groups have protested that psychological tests have been used to exclude them. Even scientifically oriented psychologists have challenged psychological testing on technical, methodological grounds. The result is that psychological testing which was once in vogue has fallen on hard times. Some sales managers look at the elimination of psychological testing as a relief from an unwelcome intrusion on their hiring decisions while others feel that the information psychological testing provided is now no longer available.

Psychological testing can provide information regarding applicants for sales jobs that cannot be obtained from other sources as economically and accurately. Motivational makeup as measured by Edwards Personal Preference, interpersonal skills as measured by Thorndike's Dimension of Temperament and the ability to think as measured by Otis are examples of information and tests that provide information uniquely available from psychological tests.

While track records or records of accomplishments can be used to judge some sales applicants, they do not exist for many minority candidates. Females, blacks and recent college graduates just don't have the track records in sales that allow you to make the judgments about sales potential that you need to make. Psychological testing is an alternative source of information which can be useful in making judgments about potential.

Certainly, minority groups rightly insist that tests be validated against criterion groups that include them. This is expensive and many companies have opted to eliminate psychological testing rather than go through the expense of validating their tests. Some have fled to the less scientifically valid Assessment Center approach. Interestingly, the same validation process required to establish the assessment criteria could be used in validating the psychological tests formerly used.

One of the major problems in using psychological tests is that they are sometimes interpreted by psychologists who have only a vague awareness of the job for which they are evaluating the person. If on the other hand, you know the psychologist-evaluator has a good knowledge of your sales job, the information provided and the recommendations made should be carefully considered. The field sales manager, however, should retain the right to make the selection decision.

Test information is as valid and as meaningful as any other source of information, including screening applications and interviews. While it may not always be completely accurate, it is nevertheless meaningful. As long as you don't make your decisions solely on the basis of the psychological tests, they can be a valuable source of information. You yourself must determine the importance of the tests, what you hope to accomplish with them, and whether or not you have the time to obtain the information they provide from other sources.

HIRING MINORITIES

The modern sales manager realizes that he or she must be involved in hiring minorities. The people who keep the records, the personnel department, and those that look at the records, agencies of the Federal government, insist that minorities be considered in all selection decisions. Sales managers must search out and find qualified applicants whether or not they apply for the sales job. This means that you must know and use minority recruitment sources. In addition, you must know how or learn how to interview and evaluate minority applicants. The recruiting sources mentioned earlier are as valid a source of minority applicants as for nonminority applicants. The interview procedures recommended earlier are also applicable.

One of the major problems managers face in hiring minority salespeople is their own attitude toward the minority. What for example is your attitude toward female sales representatives? Do you have an opinion as to how your customers will receive a black or hispanic sales representative? Is it possible for an applicant over 50 to have the high energy level needed to launch a new product? Most attitudes are the result of not understanding the minority culture.

In your search for information about applicants, you should be careful to avoid questions which can be judged to be discriminatory and not bona-fide qualifying questions. Questions about age, military experience, national origin, organizational membership, physical handicaps, religion, sex or family status are specifically prohibited in pre-employment screening. While these prohibitions may be inhibitory to the natural flow of a conversation, the point has already been made: The purpose of pre-employment screening is to uncover information about qualifications which are relevant to the job. It is thus particularly important for you when interviewing minorities to think through the real specifications for the sales job you want to fill. Questions which are job related can be asked, questions which are not job related cannot be asked. The burden of proving job relevance rests on you.

THE SELECTION DECISION

Once you have information from application forms, interviews, reference checking and possibly test results for each candidate that is applying for a job, it is time to make your selection decision.

First, you should attempt to organize your information in some relevant manner. Writing it down is one good way of organizing it. If you have been successful in obtaining information, you will have both positive and negative information for each applicant. The "positives" are strengths that will enable the applicant to do the job well; the "negatives," the weaknesses that will prevent him or her from doing so. Writing down each candidate's strengths and weaknesses makes it easier to compare qualifications. The most important thing to remember, however, is that all applicants will have some weaknesses. Similarly, they are also almost certain to have at least one or two strengths.

Since it is rare to find a perfect match between sales job and applicant, you must consider every candidate a risk. Determining the degree of risk involved, however, helps reduce selection errors. You can describe the degree of risk by establishing a rating system. Three obvious categories might be: poor, average, and good risk.

These categories should be based on how well the qualifications of the candidate meet the requirements of the job; i.e., how well you think the candidate can fill the requirements of the position. This includes knowledge, skills, experience, and personal characteristics necessary to do the job well. The final selection decision can then be a choice between applicants of stated strengths and weaknesses and of given risk rating levels.

SUMMARY: AN IMPORTANT DECISION

Finding and selecting people in most instances is left up to the field sales manager. Some managers feel that this is an unimportant responsibility compared with more important decisions that top management makes. Let's look for a minute at such responsibilities and convert these decisions on people to numbers.

On a sales team with seven members, each sales representative is responsible for one-seventh of your sales. At least one of these seven people will leave you each year if industry figures of 20 percent turnover are true for your team. That means one-seventh of your effectiveness will be determined by your ability to recruit and select applicants.

With this kind of responsibility, selecting sales team members is a particularly important decision for you. Be certain that you know the requirements; that you use every possible source of locating good applicants; that you have the greatest possible number of candidates to choose from; that you are efficient and effective in selecting the right person for the job. Doing these tasks well is one of the most difficult parts of being a successful manager—but one that pays off handsomely.

QUESTIONS THAT NEED ANSWERS

To be sure that you understand the ideas discussed in this chapter, answer the following questions:

1. Recruiting refers to finding people. Selecting refers to:
   a) eliminating people.
   b) choosing people.
   c) assigning people.
   d) interviewing people.

2. A job analysis does not include a statement of:
   a) knowledge required.
   b) personal qualities.
   c) wages paid.
   d) experience necessary.

3. When you are trying to find experienced people, the best source is:
   a) walk-ins.
   b) schools.
   c) newspapers.
   d) none of these.

4. One of the advantages of using referrals is that the applicants are:
   a) available immediately.
   b) known.
   c) experienced.
   d) prescreened.

5. The most important thing to have when you are making a selection decision is:
   a) information.
   b) test results.
   c) references.
   d) first-hand impressions.

6. An application form can:
   a) provide essential information.
   b) eliminate unqualified people.
   c) reduce interview time.
   d) all of these.

7. "Did you like your last job?" is:
   a) an open-ended question.
   b) a question that encourages a "yes" or "no" answer.
   c) a waste of time to ask.
   d) a closing question.

8. Test questions should be asked to:
   a) determine interest.
   b) give you insight.
   c) put the applicant at ease.
   d) validate an applicant's skill.

9. The "halo effect" is a term used to refer to:
   a) an applicant's religious convictions.
   b) a manager's likes or dislikes.
   c) the personal bias of both applicants and managers.
   d) none of these.

10. Checking references gives you information on an applicant's:
    a) legal status.
    b) social involvement.
    c) family status.
    d) work reputation.

If you made the following choices, you should feel that the ideas discussed are yours: 1b, 2c, 3c, 4b, 5a, 6d, 7b, 8d, 9b, 10d.

Chapter 5

Training Salespeople

CAN SELLING BE TAUGHT?

One of the oldest questions in the selling profession is whether sales skills are self-taught or learned from others. The question is best answered by defining what selling is all about. Selling can be defined as the process of influencing a buying decision. There are two sets of skills involved: interpersonal skills and communication skills. Selling skills consist of the ability to analyze another person and to present to that person a message in a convincing way. Certainly the ability to "read people" begins with our relationships with parents and peers. The use of words to convince others begins for most people at about the age of 2. Selling skills begin to develop in those that ultimately choose selling long before they start to make their living influencing the buying decisions of others. As obvious as it is that selling skills are developed early in life, it should not be concluded that selling skills cannot be taught. Basic skills can be further developed with training. Training for psychologists includes development of the skill to analyze people. Advertising professionals developed through study their skill in influencing buying decisions. When selling skills are defined as interpersonal skills and communications skills, it becomes easier to accept the idea that they are learned skills which are both self-taught and learned from others. The focus of this chapter is on the teaching process: the process of developing the skills of the people who have chosen selling as a profession.

All About a Mouse

A question frequently asked by sales managers and teachers is: How do people learn? An answer can be provided by studying one of the world's simplest learners: the mouse.

If you let a hungry mouse loose in a room, it will immediately begin to run about in search of food: It wants something.

If you have left a box of cereal in the middle of the room, the mouse will approach it and look it over: It will notice the box.

If the mouse finds that the box is open and the cover unsealed, it will lift the cover in search of food. That is, it will do something to satisfy its hunger.

The next step, of course, is obvious. The mouse will eat whatever food he finds to satisfy his hunger. So the mouse obtains food as a result of his efforts.

In much the same way as this mouse, people also learn how to act in order to reach goals. Like this mouse, people want something, notice the objects or action necessary to help them get it, do, act, or perform the necessary acts to get it, and obtain their goals as a result of their actions and efforts. They learn the steps to take to reach their desired ends.

Learning to Ride a Bicycle

Try to remember when you learned how to ride a bicycle. You wanted to learn because it looked like fun and maybe also because the other kids were riding. Your teacher put you on the bike and at first held the bike so you wouldn't fall over. This enabled you to notice how it felt to ride and balance a bike, as well as what speed was required to keep it upright. Then when your teacher let go, you pedaled hard, held the bike right and—you did it! You rode the bike all by yourself! The reward: the delights of the open road were yours. You wanted, you noticed, you performed, and you reached your goal of learning to ride a bike.

TEACHING

Now that the learning process has been pinpointed, it should be time to start teaching. Before talking about teaching, let's focus our discussion. Teaching refers to the things you do to instruct sales personnel in what to do with the products you sell. Some training can be accomplished *simply by telling* the salespeople what to do. For example, if you want to teach sales personnel where your product should be placed on a retail shelf, simply tell them it should be placed on an eye-level shelf. More complicated subjects like selling techniques or determining good floor display locations require more than simply telling. With more complex subjects and skills, it is necessary to know more about teaching and training.

Since you are responsible for training sales personnel on how to sell and merchandise your company's products, *you are a trainer during almost all of your contacts* with sales personnel. Training activities include: 1) training sales representatives during *work-withs* on the street, 2) training sales personnel during meetings. While these contacts may be brief, your skill as a trainer during these contacts will either make them beneficial learning experiences or an unprofitable investment of your time.

LEARNING HOW TO TEACH

No one can say, "I never learned a thing in my life," and very few people can say, "I never learned a thing from another person such as a teacher." Similarly, not many can say, "I never taught anybody anything." It seems strange then that this learning-teaching process eludes definition and seems both awesome and wonderful.

In the beginning of this chapter the learning process was described by four words: want, notice, act, and obtain. What about the teaching process? If your son asks you to teach him how to tie his shoes, you will do so with skill and patience.

Why then the lack of patience and time for training your people at work? Perhaps because the lessons are usually a bit more difficult, because work priorities put productivity ahead of training, and the "tell 'em" teaching method does not always work. What is needed is a simple method that can be used at work with difficult as well as simple learning tasks, a teaching method that takes relatively little time and goes beyond just "tell 'em."

THE THREE-STEP METHOD FOR ON-THE-JOB TEACHING

The three-step method is an easy to learn teaching method that can be used to teach all kinds of sales and merchandising lessons. It is a teaching method that is not time consuming and one that can be used in all situations even when the person being taught may not want to accept the need for training.

Step 1: Tell and Show

The first step is to tell sales representatives what you want done. In other words, explain what you want done and then demonstrate how it is to be done. An example should make this point clear. As a sales manager you want to teach one of your sales representatives how to sell the holiday floor display program.

You begin by saying,

Jim, I want to go over some suggestions for selling holiday displays with you as we work together today. I've found that sales representatives sell displays when they remember just four things. First, choose a good location ahead of time. Second, start the conversation by showing the display card and then talk about the seasonal appeal of the products. Third, suggest a given number of cases. Fourth, convert the cases to total profit. Let me show you what I mean on the next call.

With the sales representative, look around the store at the various display locations and choose a good location as well as several alternative locations. Then, make the pitch so the sales representative can see what you want done.

> You: "Dale, what do you think of this display card?"
> Retailer: "It looks good."
> You: "It'll look real good on top of the holiday display."
> Retailer: "I thought so, it's that time of year."
> You: "I'd like to suggest that you display twenty cases and that you put it on the end of the aisle near the cold box. Twenty cases will make you over $150 in profit. Should the order be heavy on the small or large sizes?"
> Retailer: "Go heavy on the large sizes."

To reassure yourself that the learner understands what you want done, ask him to tell you what he is going to do or say before you ask for a solo performance. The sales representative should be able to tell you the four things that you want done.

1. Choose a spot ahead of time.
2. Show the card and mention the seasonal appeal.
3. Suggest the number of cases needed on the display.
4. Convert the cases to total profit.

Step 2: Rehearse and Observe

You have told the learner what you want him to do, you have shown him what you want him to do, now he needs to start doing it. Before you ask him to perform under real life conditions, take time to rehearse under realistic but safe conditions.

> In our example, ask the sales representative to make the floor display pitch to you in the car before he makes the pitch to the retailer in the store.
> You: "Tell me about the retailer."
> Sales representative: "He's strictly a facts and figures retailer; profit is his big thing."
> You: "OK, I'll play the part of the retailer and you make the floor display pitch to me."
> Sales Representative: "How's this for an *expensive* display card? . . ."

Rehearsing is nothing more than role playing under safe conditions. Through rehearsing, you can help the sales representative correct his mistakes before they are made in a situation that could embarrass him.

Following the role playing in the car, go with the sales representative into the store and observe the presentation. Watch without interrupting. This is the only way you will know what the sales representative can do under realistic conditions. Save your evaluation and comments until after you leave the store.

Sales Representative: "How's this for an
expensive display card?"
Retailer: "Looks great. . . ."

In Step 2, you ask the learner to rehearse under safe conditions and then perform under real life conditions while you observe.

Step 3: Review and Recognize

In Step 3, you review what you saw the learner do and recognize what was done right as well as what was done wrong. In our example, you would review how you saw the pitch on the holiday floor display and then through discussion point out what was done right and what was done wrong.

THE CURBSTONE CONFERENCE

Since Step 3 usually takes place in the car after you leave the retail account, it has become known as the "curbstone conference." A few thoughts on conducting "Curbstone" are presented below:

Ask Before You Tell

Have the sales representative give an appraisal of his performance before you give yours. Give him an opportunity to point out his own errors and his own successes before you tell him what you think.

Start Your Comments on a Positive Note

Begin your review of his performance by saying something positive what he did. This is important if the sales representative is to make the distinction between what he did right and wrong. After hearing some praise, the criticism comes easier.

Use the WE Approach

Let the sales representative know that you identify with him by using the word "we" rather than "you." For example, "How can we handle that objection if it comes up again?" rather than, "How can you handle it?"

KISMIF = Keep It Simple, Make It Fun

Don't overwhelm the sales representative with a dozen points of criticism. Stress a few important points, help him to realize his mistakes and do it in such a way that he will realize that it is not the end of the world if he doesn't do everything you want him to do on the first try.

Ask for a Restatement

Get some response from the sales representative that indicates that he really grasped the points you made. Ask for a restatement of the positives as well as the negatives.

PRACTICE EXERCISE: Using the Curbstone Technique

You and your sales representative, Sam Song, have just left an account owned by John Johnson. Sam just made a pitch on distribution of one of your products using facts and figures about our advertising support. Mr. Johnson didn't buy and even seemed annoyed that Sam would bother him with all those confusing numbers. After leaving the store, Sam turns to you and says, "How can you discuss the impact of advertising with an idiot like that?" Outline your response to Sam's question in the space provided below.

_____

_____

_____

_____

_____

_____

_____

_____

_____

Summary: Three Step Method

Whether you are trying to teach an experienced sales representative how to make more efficient calls or a new sales representative how to merchandise products on the shelf, the three-step training method will be useful. First, tell the learner what you want him to do, then show him how to do it. Once you think he has grasped the lesson, rehearse with him under safe conditions and then watch as he performs the task in a real situation. After he has performed the task—merchandised a shelf—review what you saw him do and recognize what he did right and what he did wrong.

FIVE TRAINING PRINCIPLES

Psychologists have spent lifetimes trying to discover the laws of learning. For the most part, generalizations have been denied by obvious exceptions and even today, there are no generally accepted laws of learning. A law is something that is always true; a principle, on the other hand, is generally true but not always. Most psychologists admit that there are, however, about five principles of learning which can effectively be used by trainers. These are stated as sales training principles.

Principle 1: Determine what you want the sales representative to learn before you start teaching.

Vague, unspecific goals lead to vague, unspecific results. Know what you want to teach and base the content and technique on this goal.

Principle 2: Don't try to teach everything in one lesson.

Establish a training schedule that will allow you to take one subject at a time. Give the learner an opportunity to absorb one lesson at a time. Don't try to cram everything down his throat in one long lesson. (Spaced learning is to be preferred to massed learning.)

Principle 3: Build on what is known.

Determine what he knows that will help him learn what you want him to learn. Use the things he knows to help you teach him. Also, be aware of the things that he knows that will interfere with his learning. (Positive and negative transfer.)

Principle 4: Don't be afraid to repeat yourself.

For knowledge to be learned and retained, the learner must be exposed to it several times and study it in its different applications. Repeating yourself is necessary if learning is to take place. Hopefully, you can vary your message slightly, but whether you can or not, you must tell it, retell it and tell it again. (Repetition creates awareness.)

Principle 5: Get the learner involved.

Learners must become involved in the learning process, must participate in the learning if it is to take place. When the learner has the opportunity to talk about the material, ask questions, discuss the content of the material read and put into practice, he will learn the lesson more readily and apply it more frequently. (Principle of participation.)

WHAT IS THE LESSON TO BE LEARNED?

If you are working for a company that has set training programs, you are indeed lucky. The company training programs outline the lessons to be learned and usually suggest how you should teach the lessons.

If you are with a company without set training programs, you must build the programs yourself. Start with a clear statement of what you want to train the person to do. Whether you are teaching a sales rep how to use a new form or teaching him to personalize his presentations, be specific about the behavior you want to shape.

After you have determined the end result you hope to achieve, then ask yourself the question, "What knowledge and skills are required to do this?" After you have given some thought and time to these prerequisites, your lesson will become clear.

ORGANIZE THE LESSON TO MAKE IT EASIER TO LEARN

Once the lesson has been stated or written down, look for ways of organizing it so that it will be easier to learn. What should be taught first? Can parts of the lesson be grouped together for easier learning? What are the key points? Where should the lesson be taught?

Let's consider an example. As a sales manager of route sales representatives, you are interested in having them run their routes profitably. The lesson of running a route profitably could well contain hundreds of items. For example: Control your sales, give a receipt for money, insist on being checked into a store, organize your sales receipts as you go through the day. The best way to present a lesson like this is to organize the lesson in terms of what needs to be done in the morning before checking out, the procedure to be followed on each call and the system of checking in at night.

Organizing a lesson in terms of the sequence in which it is performed makes more sense to the learner than jumping from one point on a list to another unrelated point.

ADAPT THE LESSON TO THE LEARNER

Training programs—whether ones you personally have developed or more general programs prepared by other firms—are developed for groups of people rather than for individuals. Hopefully, they are developed with a knowledge of the job and an image of the typical person who will be trained for that job. What happens, however, when you hire an experienced salesperson who already knows many of the things contained in the standard training programs? Obviously, the lesson must be revised so that it suits the more experienced salesperson.

If a learner already knows the information or has the skill required for the job, training in these areas is unnecessary. An experienced salesperson, for example, usually knows how to get retailers' attention. How much he knows can be determined by watching and talking with him.

The process of adapting the lesson to the individual is shown below:

Knowledge and skill required. (The basic lesson)	–	Knowledge and skill possessed by the learner.	=	Knowledge and skill to be learned. (The learner's lesson)

In order to adapt the lesson to the learner, you must first find out what he knows. Then you can go on to teach him what he doesn't know.

PRACTICE EXERCISE: Developing a Lesson Plan

You have just hired a new sales representative for one of your key territories. The new sales representative, Kathy Wyler, has sold crackers and cookies in the supermarket setting but she has never sold your kind of product.

1. What is the lesson to be learned?

_____

_____

_____

_____

2. How can the lesson be organized for ease of learning?

_____

_____

_____

_____

3. How would you modify the lesson if you also hired another sales rep who had no selling experience but knew your product?

_____

_____

TRAINING SCHEDULES

While basic orientation can be accomplished in several weeks of concentrated training, most training beyond the basics requires managers to make commitments which are spread out over weeks and months. The only way that a sales manager can keep track of the training needs of the sales representatives and do something about them is to develop a schedule for each of the salespeople which states the training needs—the lessons to be learned and specific time for meeting these training needs. An example is presented below:

| | Name: Frank Simons | | |
TOPIC	TIME REQUIRED	SCHEDULED	COMPLETED
Product knowledge training	1 Day	10 Oct. 25 Oct.	10 Oct.
Sell distribution	1½ Days	15 Oct.	15 Oct.
Place mistake-proof sales orders	1 Hour	After Work 13 Oct.	13 Oct.

TRAINING TOOLS: MAKING LESSONS MORE INTERESTING

The simplest form of training involves a manager telling and showing the learner what to do. For some lessons, that is all that is needed. For many lessons, though, simple telling and showing takes too much time and is dull. This is the time when training tools can be used effectively. Training tools make learning quicker, easier and more interesting. Charts, job cards, pamphlets, manuals, movies and slides are some of the more frequently used training tools.

Sources of Training Tools

The following companies are some of the many companies that sell training tools specifically designed for the field sales managers:

- Dartnell Corporation
  4660 Ravenswood Avenue
  Chicago, Illinois 60640
- Rountable Films
  113 North Sanvincente Boulevard
  Beverly Hills, California 90211
- Creative Media, Inc.
  820 Keosauqua Way
  Des Moines, Iowa 50309

Making Your Own Training Tools

When it is not possible to buy ready-made training tools, make some of your own. It is a lot easier to develop your own training tools than most people think. Typewriters and copy machines, for example, can be used to put words into print. Learners can study the printed words at their own speed while they wait for you and at home. Or, you might use lettering sets like the ones kids use to help you to make posters. Occasionally you may also find an amateur artist who likes to do simple illustrations. Most will do them free.

If tapes are available, you might want to record the lesson, which can be played back on a tape recorder by the learner even when you aren't available. Since tape recorders are available in most sales organizations and can be used economically, you can tape the lessons at your leisure and have the learner play them back on his own.

Polaroid snapshots of actual work scenes and pictures from magazines can also be used to make lessons come alive. Since home movie cameras and slide projectors are common, you might also be able to make your own slides and movies.

The following are a few examples of manager-made training tools.

The Pocket Card

One of the most useful training tools that can be developed easily is the pocket card. One field sales manager was having difficulty teaching the sales representatives to use a set procedure for selling retailers shelf changes. He answered this training need by typing the suggested procedure on a card and asked the sales representatives to carry the card in their pockets and review it whenever they were about to make a shelf change pitch. The card looked like the following:

SELLING SHELF CHANGES

1. Prepare a sketch of the retailer's current shelf setup. (The current version.)
2. Analyze the retailer's current arrangement and space allocation on the shelf.
3. Develop a proposal for changing the retailer space allocation and/or arrangement.
4. Prepare a sketch of the proposal. (The after version.)
5. Use the sketches to sell the proposal to the retailer.

Using the pocket card helped the sales manager to teach the procedure and the sales team's score in selling shelf changes improved significantly.

The Poster

A poster like the one below solved the training problem for another manager who was having difficulty clarifying the notion of reach-level shelf locations for his products.

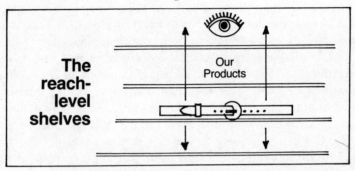

Did someone say, "A picture is worth a thousand words"? Let's summarize this section on making your own training tools with a simple outline.

How to Develop Your Own Training Tools:

1. Words.
   a. Printed with a typewriter.
   b. Reproduced on a copy machine.
   c. Printed on posters.
   d. Recorded on a tape recorder.
2. Pictures.
   a. Taken with cameras.
      1. Snapshots.
      2. Slides.
      3. Home movies.
   b. Cut from magazines.

BACK TO THE MOUSE

Your people learn in much the same way the mouse learned.

Want: If a sales representative does not want to learn, and if you cannot motivate him to learn, he will not learn. A salesperson who does not want to learn listening skills will waste your training efforts.

Notice: In order to learn a person must first notice what he needs to learn. A sales representative may not realize, for example, that he does not listen. He therefore needs to recognize his weakness and become aware of how he can overcome it.

Act: When the learner has noticed what he should, he must try the skill. The sales representative must force himself to pay attention to the retailer's comments. Pointing out problems is ineffective unless the sales representative starts listening.

Obtain: If the learner starts to benefit from listening more he will continue to do it. When he discovers the usefulness of retailers' involvement to make more sales, he will listen. If this goal is important to him, he will reinforce his own behavior so that the next time he makes a presentation, he will listen as well as speak.

Our discussion of how to teach has taken us from the mouse learner to the human learner. Since the learning process and training method have been explained, it is time to tie the two together. The following chart will help you connect the two concepts.

What Trainer Does	What Learner Does	Why
Plan the lesson—what and how to do something.		To help learner want to learn.
Adapt the lesson to the learner.		
Tell the learner about the lesson.	Listens or reads.	To help learner notice how to perform lesson.
Show the learner about the lesson.	Watches.	
Rehearse the lesson with the learner.	Works under safe conditions.	To help learner apply lesson.
Observe the learner performing the lesson.	Works under real conditions.	
Reward/recognize the learner's achievements.	Feels satisfied.	To help learner recognize the goals that are reached—what and how.
Follow-up on the lesson at a later date.	Works on the job.	

THE TRAINING MEETING: A DISCUSSION, NOT A LECTURE

So far our discussions have focused on the one-on-one training method. There are occasions, however, when a manager has to train groups of people. Many managers are frankly afraid of training meetings or classes. This is because they feel they have to use extensive notes and be more prepared about the subject than anyone else who attends. That's a big order and requires time and talent that most managers don't have.

There is an alternative to the lecture, however. It's called the discussion conference. In the discussion conference, the manager simply introduces the topic to be discussed, keeps everybody talking about the designated subject, asks questions to stimulate discussion, and periodically summarizes the discussion. He is not the answer man. Like any other member of the group, he expresses opinions that are open to discussion. His preparation time is limited to deciding how to introduce the training topics and what kind of questions will get the discussion started and keep it going.

Another big advantage of the discussion conference is that it enables everybody to participate. Both junior and senior members can express their opinions in open discussion. Since all members are encouraged to contribute, no one has to have all the answers. The point of the discussion is to give everyone an opportunity to say what he thinks about the topic and hopefully to come to solutions or recognitions as a result of mutual agreement and teamwork.

Let's take an example. The lesson to be learned is how to overcome objections to cold box placement of small sizes of your product. The discussion conference leader would begin the group training experience by listing the topic to be discussed on a blackboard or an easel pad. Then he would begin asking questions like:

1) How could the objection "I need my cold box space for other products" be overcome?

2) What would you say to a retailer who claims that the turnover on small sizes is too slow to deserve cold box space?

3) How would you handle the suburban type of account that objects to cold box space for your product because it attracts rowdy people?

This type of question gets the discussion going and all the discussion conference leader has to do is control the discussion and periodically summarize what has been said.

Preparation for the Discussion Conference

Decide on a limited topic. Don't try to discuss everything in one conference, it can't be done. The topic "Overcoming objections to cold box distribution for your products" is a limited and manageable topic. "Increasing Distribution of Your Products on the Shelf, the Floor and in the Cold Box," would be beyond the limits of one discussion conference.

Decide how to introduce the topic. One way to introduce a topic is to announce it and then review the importance and relevance of the topic. Another way to introduce a discussion topic is to show a movie on the topic—for example, the movie *Overcoming Objections* could be used to introduce the topic mentioned in our example. The points made in the movie are specific enough that a discussion of the points as they relate to "Cold Box Space for Your Product" could result. Role playing is another way to introduce a topic. In this approach, the topic to be discussed is presented by two people playing simulated roles. In our example, one member of the group could play the role of a beach-area retailer with no space for your product and another participant could play the role of sales representative. The role playing situation focuses the attention on the desired topic and gets discussion going.

Develop discussion questions. Since questions stimulate discussion, they should be thought out ahead of time. The three types of questions that result in the most discussion are:

1. The Overhead Questions
2. Pointed Questions
3. Problem Situation Questions

An overhead question is one that is asked of the whole group. In our earlier example—"How could the objection: 'I need my cold box space for more profitable products' be overcome?"—is an overhead question. The pointed question is one that is asked of a specific person. "Harry, what would you say to a retailer who says turnover is too slow on your products to deserve cold box space?" The third type of discussion question is a problem situation question. This type of question asks about a real life situation with which all of the group in the meeting are familiar. The "suburban" question presented in the opening example is such a question. If you take the time to develop discussion questions, you can be assured of a successful training conference.

Conducting the Conference

As suggested earlier, start the conference by writing the topic to be discussed on the blackboard or on an easel and indicate to the group that this is the topic to be discussed and ask everybody to stick with the topic. Introduce the topic and then get the discussion started and keep it going by asking questions. Use the questions you prepared ahead of time and encourage the members of the group to interact with each other.

Keep the meeting under control. Keep the meeting under control by insisting that a group discussion be held rather than a discussion between one or two members. Side conversations should be discouraged and all comments should be presented to the group as a whole. Also, be sure to direct the group back to the stated discussion topic if it strays off the main course of discussion.

Periodically summarize the discussion. You should also periodically summarize the discussion so that the members of the discussion group will feel that the discussion has led to some conclusions. This can be done verbally or on the blackboard. When you summarize, more questions are stimulated.

Like any other skill, discussion conference leadership is not learned overnight. You need to practice conducting discussion conferences before the skill will be yours.

PRACTICE EXERCISE: Discussion Conference

Choose a topic for a training-oriented discussion conference. Develop questions to start, stimulate and encourage discussion.

Topic: _____

_____

_____

Overhead Questions: _____

_____

_____

_____

Pointed Questions: _____

_____

_____

_____

Problem-Situation Questions: _____

_____

_____

_____

USING ROLE PLAYING IN A TRAINING MEETING

Role playing at its best simulates a real life situation and offers the salesperson an opportunity to practice or rehearse a sales presentation under conditions where his peers can observe his presentation and where the consequences of his presentation are not irreversible. The purpose of role playing is to help salespeople improve the sales presentations they make.

Because of past experience with role playing, you probably know that role playing does not always help people learn and improve their skills. Role playing can be nothing more than an unnecessary embarrassment for the salesperson playing the role and a waste of time for those watching. There are, however, some things that can be done to insure that role playing will shape behavior and help salespeople learn.

Role Playing Rules:

- Allow each salesperson to prepare the sales presentation in advance.
- Review the main sales points that should be made in the presentation before the role playing begins.
- Carefully define the role of retailer and salesperson just before the role playing begins.
- Record the sales presentation as it is being made.
- Keep the actual role playing session brief.
- Involve all of the observers in the sales presentation.
- Discuss the sales presentation in a critical yet constructive manner.

Allow Each Salesperson to Prepare in Advance

To avoid embarrassing participants, give them advance notice and suggest that they spend some time preparing for the role playing in advance. This can be done in several ways: (1) announce the sales proposal and suggest salespeople think about it before the meeting and (2) ask the salespeople to write out the role playing assignment and bring it to the meeting. In addition, there is some merit in informing the first role player in advance that they will be the "first up."

Review the Main Sales Points

Since the purpose of role playing is to practice delivering the message, time should not be wasted developing the message during the actual role playing. With the help of the salespeople, outline the key sales points on an easel pad or blackboard or break up into teams and let each team define the message before the role playing begins.

Define the Roles

Roles of sales representative and retailer can be defined by verbally outlining each role. A more effective method is to outline each role on a 3 × 5 index card, read it to the meeting participants and give it to the role players to use during the role playing session. Cue cards outlining roles which both players and meeting participants can see produces some of the most interesting role playing sessions.

Definition of the retailer's role should include his identity; the type of store run, typical objections he raises and some indication of his personality. The sales representative can either play himself or some other person who you define.

Record the Sales Presentation

As the sales presentation is being made, it should be recorded by the meeting leader. This can be done by recording in writing the key words used by the retailer and sales representative. The key words help you focus on the delivery and the exchange of words but it leaves out some of the dialogue. A complete record of the dialogue can be made on an audio tape recorder or both words and visual can be captured on videotape.

Keep the Actual Role Playing Session Brief

Five- to ten-minute presentations seem best. More people can be involved with brief role playing sessions and there is still time to discuss them.

Involve All of the Observers

Role playing is most effective when everybody is involved. Suggestions for getting involvement include asking each observer to complete a critique sheet. For example: How did he get attention? What benefits did he mention? Did he overcome all objections? How did he close? The team preparation of the message mentioned before also insures total observer participation. The team representative makes the presentation and the observers are involved with their team representative.

Discuss Critically Yet Constructively

Unless you are willing to evaluate critically your sales representatives' presentations and suggest or develop ways for making better presentations, role playing should be avoided. Most people who call themselves sales representatives think they can sell; they can. The point is that they can become better, and critically yet constructively examining role playing is one way to do it.

THE SELF-TEACHING APPROACH

Because of time demands on managers, some sales organizations have turned to the self-teaching approach to training. With this method the learner teaches himself using one of the following techniques:

- Texts and workbooks
- Programmed instruction texts
- Films and videotapes

Texts and workbooks which are a part of home study courses are ideal for self-teaching. The texts have the necessary information, and the workbooks give the learners an opportunity to use and apply it. In addition to reducing the time a manager needs to spend in training, the advantage of this approach is that no special equipment or training is needed.

Programmed instruction texts are written to make it easy for the learner to learn by himself. Information is presented in short paragraphs followed by several questions with answers which the learner can check. If he answers correctly, his answer is reinforced, and he is assured that he knows the information. If his answer is incorrect, however, his mistake is explained and he must go back and try again to answer the question correctly.

While learning is virtually assured if the learner tries to learn, programmed texts are sometimes boring, because they assume that the learner has no information. They therefore present all information one step at a time. For more experienced employees, this can be tedious and a waste of time.

Films and videotapes can be used for self-instruction through the use of video-cassette players and a regular TV screen or a front screen automatic projector. The equipment varies in cost from $300 to $900. The learner sits in front of the screen and watches and listens to the tape. He can replay any part of the tape again and is expected to complete an accompanying student workbook. The obvious advantage of this approach is that it is an interesting and fun way to learn.

All three of these approaches help the learner to learn. But remember: In order for any of them to be effective, the manager must become involved in the process and must help the learner to apply what has been learned to the job.

TRAINING NEW SALESPEOPLE

It would indeed be a delight to train new salespeople if there were no time limits and if you were the only teacher. Unfortunately, as field sales manager, you will seldom have this luxury. Usually, your training will be limited to one day work-withs and you will be one of many of the people from whom the new salesperson learns. The big danger in training new salespeople is in assuming they know nothing and trying to teach everything in too short a period of time.

The answer to training new salespeople is:
- work with the new sales representative as soon after he is employed as is possible. If you do, he will learn the right way to sell your product from the beginning.
- find out what the sales representative knows and determine the skills he has before you begin to teach. Determining training needs, as has been pointed out, avoids assuming knowledge and skills and also prevents talking down to a knowledgeable and skilled person.
- once you have determined what the sales representative needs to learn, don't try to teach him everything in one day. It is much better to concentrate on one or two lessons that can be learned in the time available.

SUMMARY: TRAINING SHAPES BEHAVIOR

Training refers to the things you do to instruct sales personnel what you want them to do and how it can be done. You are a trainer during almost all of your contacts with sales personnel. A three-step method of teaching was presented: 1) Tell and Show, 2) Rehearse and Observe, 3) Review and Recognize. Defining and adapting lessons was discussed briefly. The dangers of trying to teach new salespeople everything you know in one training session was pointed out. The discussion conference and role playing approach to training groups of salespeople was presented and suggestions for using these techniques were made.

QUESTIONS THAT NEED ANSWERS

To be sure that you understand the ideas discussed in this chapter, answer the following questions.

1. The teaching method recommended for use by field sales managers has:
   a) 6 steps.
   b) 5 steps.
   c) 4 steps.
   d) 3 steps.

2. Planning the lesson involves:
   a) determining the lesson to be learned.
   b) organizing the lesson.
   c) making the lesson interesting.
   d) all of these.

3. Training tools:
   a) should be developed by headquarters.
   b) are of questionable value.
   c) require expensive equipment.
   d) can be developed on a limited budget.

4. Tell and show mean the same thing as:
   a) explain and demonstrate.
   b) rehearse and observe.
   c) teach and perform.
   d) job review and job performance.

5. The purpose of rehearsing is to give the learner an opportunity to do the work task under:
   a) safe conditions.
   b) real life conditions.
   c) your supervision.
   d) all of these.

6. Adapting the lesson to the learner is important because some learners:
   a) are too slow to learn if you don't adapt the lesson.
   b) resent teachers.
   c) already know some of the things they need to know.
   d) speak a different language.

7. The key to an effective discussion conference is to:
   a) have an answer man available.
   b) ask the right questions.
   c) invite the right people.
   d) start on time.

8. The biggest problem in training new people is to try to teach them:
   a) too much too soon.
   b) too little too late.
   c) both of the above.
   d) none of the above.

If you made the following choices, you should feel that the ideas discussed are yours: 1d, 2d, 3d, 4a, 5a, 6c, 7b, 8c.

Chapter 6

Evaluating and Improving Performance

HOW AM I DOING, BOSS?

Even though salespeople are basically independent workers and the results of their work easily seen, they still like to know what you think of their performance. As team leader, it's your job to answer the question, "How am I doing, boss?" In this chapter, two topics will be covered: rating or evaluating sales performance and telling a sales representative how you rated him so that his performance will improve.

TRAINING AND IMPROVING

Training usually refers to teaching a sales representative something new. When a sales representative starts on the job, almost everything is new. When you introduce a system like a new telephone ordering system, you are teaching sales representatives of all experience levels something new. Improvement, on the other hand, usually refers to becoming better at something, acquiring skills and knowledge beyond the bare minimal needed to perform the job. The major difference between training and improving is that training involves shaping behavior and developing or improving usually means changing behavior.

IMPROVEMENT MEANS CHANGE

One of the biggest problems sales managers face in trying to improve the performance of their sales representatives is resistance to change. Most sales representatives have developed set ways of doing things and improvement plans are met with self-protective resistance to change. What you call an improvement plan the sales representative must view as a program of change. The characteristic human response to change is resistance. A sales representative may think, for example, that the way he sells bookings for floor displays works most of the time, so why should he change? From your point of view, his set ways must change. The experienced sales representative resists improvement plans primarily because improvement plans mean changing.

Change
- Implies criticism
- Produces fear
- Upsets a pattern

Change suggests that what the sales representative is currently doing is wrong. Change implies criticism. The sales representative says to himself, What is wrong with the way I'm currently selling floor displays? My score is not perfect but I do sell some. In suggesting that the sales representative change his approach to retailers in selling floor displays, you inevitably imply criticism of what he is currently doing.

Like all people, salespeople fear the unknown. A recommendation to change represents a recommendation to use an unknown system or experiment with the use of an unfamiliar skill. A sales representative who changes his behavior as you suggest he should is gambling with sales results. He may not be successful in using the new system or skill.

Almost all of the things we do at work are interrelated. The sales representative may have to re-route his territory in order to call on a major account when the decision maker is in the store. Re-routing will force the sales representative into changing a set pattern of doing things. Change upsets a pattern.

Resistance to change can be overcome if you:
- Start with a review of *goals* the salesperson wants to reach and then focus the discussion on the methods used to reach these goals.
- *Suggest* different methods of reaching goals by referring to the way other salespeople do things.
- Use work—with experiences as examples.

Whenever a sales representative feels that your discussion is focusing on a goal that he really wants to reach and is having difficulty reaching, it will be easier for you to suggest change and to bring about improvement without threatening. Let's say, for example a sales representative wants to gain distribution on the small sizes of your product. He has not succeeded in gaining the desired distribution. Once he has admitted that a goal he wants to reach is not being reached, you are in a position to discuss alternative ways of doing it. You have created the need to change.

Suggesting new and different ways of doing things, suggesting alternate methods is much easier when you refer to the way other sales representatives are doing things. This is particularly effective when the salesperson you are trying to change looks on the other representatives as successful. For example, you want the salesperson to change the way he makes retail calls. By referring to the call pattern used by another sales representative you will find it much easier to present your ideas. It is easier for most people to accept third-party testimony than it is to accept a direct recommendation from a boss.

If the sales manager and sales representative have worked together, calling on stores, they have common experiences which they can talk about. These experiences make the sales representative more open to suggestion because he has the feeling that the sales manager has some understanding of the problems which are uniquely his. The successes and failures which were commonly experienced on the street together will serve as the basis for meaningful conversation when suggestions for improvement are discussed.

THE NEED FOR PERFORMANCE EVALUATION

To many managers it may seem strange to consider rating or evaluating sales performance since the success or failure of a sales representative consists of meeting or not meeting sales goals. Shouldn't a sales representative be rated solely on the basis of his sales? Meeting case sales goals is only a part of the performance record. In the consumer products industry, merchandising goals such as shelf placement and floor displays are equally important. Goals are also only a part of the record. Governmental regulations and budgets suggest that the methods used to reach goals, and the resources required to reach goals are also important. Evaluation of performance should include an examination of both what was sold and how it was sold.

In order to evaluate effectively performance of a sales team member, you and the sales representative must have a clear understanding of what his goals are and how they should be reached.

EVALUATION BEGINS WITH A PERFORMANCE ORIENTED JOB DESCRIPTION

A job description should answer the question, "What am I responsible for doing and how am I supposed to do it?" That is to say, a job description should contain a statement of accountability —the goals to be reached and a statement of the system or procedure to be followed to reach the goals. An example of this type of job description is presented on the next page:

JOB DESCRIPTION: SALES REPRESENTATIVE—SPICES

The sales representative is expected to help store managers sell his products to consumers by: Merchandising shelves, building displays, selling convincingly and planning.

Merchandising Shelves

Recommends an appropriate selection and the right quantity of products for each store.
Knows where each of his products should be on the shelf.
Chooses the most advantageous position for his products.
Determines accurately the number of facings each product needs.
Places and services extenders, tie-ins and second locations.
Uses channel markers, price tags and shelf extenders.
Can convince store managers to make necessary shelf changes.
Services the shelf regularly: fills, faces, cleans and re-orders.

Building and Maintaining Floor Displays

Chooses good locations for each of his floor displays.
Can sell store managers on displaying his products.
Knows when to use a case stack, a rack and a bin.
Uses signs with price and message cards on displays.
Services and maintains each floor display.

Selling Convincingly

Knows how to get managers to pay attention.
Talks clearly and convincingly about new products, promotions and shelf changes.
Can prove what he says and overcome objections if they are raised.
Knows how to close a sales conversation by making it easy for the manager to say "yes."

Planning The Work

Follows a set procedure on each store call.
Completes reports and records in a timely and accurate manner.
Sets specific account goals for promotions and introduction of new products.

The job description suggests that there are four performance areas to be rated: shelf merchandising, floor display activity, selling conversations and account and territory planning. The description of each of these activities presented in the job description helps clarify what the sales representative is to do and how it is to be done. Planning, for example, includes: following a set call procedure, completing reports and keeping records and setting and reaching specific account goals.

HOW CAN THESE PERFORMANCE GOALS BE MEASURED?

The next question that should be asked is: How can these be measured? Each of these performance areas must be judged on knowledge of accomplishments made in the territory. This means knowledge of accomplishments in each account. While surveying in-store conditions for your products on the shelf and on the floor will allow you to rate the sales representative on two of these areas, shelf merchandising and floor display activity; the only way to rate a sales representative's selling skill is to observe him while he is selling. Some inference can be made about selling from the results, but a critical evaluation of selling skills requires personal observation. The same is true of in-store call procedure; it must be observed to be rated. Record keeping and planning for sales promotions can be evaluated by looking at the sales representative's books and plans on or off the street.

While it is probably not possible to have an exact numerical rating, some numerical evaluations can be made by counting the number of stores in which a sales representative meets the performance standards. For example, the representative followed the call pattern in 9 out of 10 stores. Displays were up to standard in 6 out of 10 stores. The same can be said for case sales goals for products by size.

Job descriptions which state the goals to be reached and indicate the methods to be used to reach these goals can serve as the basis for evaluating the performance of team members.

CONVERTING JOB DESCRIPTIONS INTO EVALUATION FORMS

Based on performance goals stated in the job description, the rating form becomes a tool for evaluating each team member and helps insure that consistent, meaningful performance criteria are used by the manager of the team. An example of this type of rating form is presented below:

PERFORMANCE EVALUATION

Name: _____ Territory: _____ Date: _____

Length of Service: _____ Date of Last Evaluation _____

Evaluator: _____ Date of Next Evaluation _____
   1 = Excellent   2 = Good   3 = Satisfactory   4 = Unsatisfactory

(1) *Merchandising Shelves:* .... 1. 2. 3. 4.
Supporting Comments: _____
   Major Strength: _____
   Major Improvement Need: _____

(2) *Floor Displays:* .... 1. 2. 3. 4.
Supporting Comments: _____
   Major Strength: _____
   Major Improvement Need: _____

(3) *Selling:* .... 1. 2. 3. 4.
Supporting Comments: _____
   Major Strength: _____
   Major Improvement Need: _____

(4) *Planning:* .... 1. 2. 3. 4.
Supporting Comments: _____
   Major Strength: _____
   Major Improvement Need: _____

At the top of the form, identifying information is presented. Then each of the performance areas is given a separate rating. Each rating is supported by comments and a statement of major strengths and major improvement needs. A sales manager might cite, for example, servicing shelves as the sales representative's major strength and convincing store managers to change shelves as the major improvement need. These observations are followed by supporting comments.

The numerical rating on the form consists of a judgment of Excellent (1), Good (2), Satisfactory (3), Unsatisfactory (4). While this numerical rating is subjective, it does force a sales manager to make a decision on how he sees the sales representative's performance in the area being rated.

What Is Good or Excellent?

Sales managers sometimes ask the question, "What is good or excellent?" The best answer to this question is: "It's good if you think it is good!" The performance evaluation form is not designed to be a scientifically precise instrument; it is designed to be a subjectively meaningful tool. It is a tool to be used by the sales manager doing the rating. When all is said and done, your rating and comments represent your opinion of the salesperson you rated. It should be used as a tool to assist you in evaluating and developing your own salespeople.

In companies where performance evaluations become a part of the sales representative's personnel record, the ratings should be modified to include the impression of the person you wish to communicate to the company.

PRACTICE EXERCISE: Interpreting a Performance Evaluation

The following performance evaluation was completed on sales representative Craig Gong. Craig is a distributor sales representative who sells wines to grocery and liquor stores.

(1) *Territory Management* .... 1. **②** 3. 4.
Supporting Comments: Craig is aware of sales trends in his area and credit status of his accounts.

    Major Strength: Excellent use and maintenance of route books.

    Major Improvement Need: Pre-plan more effectively for in-store improvements.

(2) *Selling:* ....1. 2. **③** 4.
Supporting Comments: _____

    Major Strength: In accounts where he is liked, he asks and gets.

    Major Improvement Need: Craig tends to depend too much on rapport sales and should work on building more factual sales presentations.

(3) *Merchandising:* .... 1. 2. **③** 4.
Support Comments: _____

    Major Strength: Merchandising in smaller accounts.

    Major Improvement Need: Floor displays and shelf point of sale in large accounts.

(4) *Servicing:* .... 1. 2. **③** 4.
Supporting Comments: Takes accurate inventories and writes mistake-proof orders.

    Major Strength: Giving customers personal attention with problems.

    Major Improvement Need: _____

(5) *Administrative:* .... 1. **②** 3. 4.
Supporting Comments: Reports submitted by Craig are generally accurate and legible.

    Major Strength: Thoroughness of reports.

    Major Improvement Need: Reports must be submitted on time. (Daily reports mailed daily.)

Questions about Craig Gong:

1. What are the performance areas that concern you most?

_____
_____
_____

2. Do numerical ratings (2 = Good, 3 = Satisfactory) make sense in terms of the stated strengths, weaknesses and comments?

_____
_____
_____

3. What evidence is there that the sales manager rating Craig Gong really knows how he performs?

_____
_____
_____

PERFORMANCE IMPROVEMENT CONFERENCE

Once you have evaluated a sales representative, you have the information you need to discuss his performance. The evaluation or rating can then be discussed with the sales representative and used by you and he or she in developing an improvement plan.

While it is possible to discuss your evaluation of a sales representative with him while you work with him on the street or to discuss it with him in a casual conversation before or after a meeting, it is very difficult to bring about any real meaningful change unless you take the time to discuss your evaluation and develop an improvement plan in a private conversation or conference with the sales representative. These conversations have come to be known as performance improvement conferences.

The purpose of the performance improvement conference is to:
- Discuss the sales representative's performance.
- Isolate performance area needing improvement.
- Help the sales representative develop an improvement plan that will help him reach some of the goals he is not currently reaching.

ATTITUDES TOWARD PERFORMANCE
IMPROVEMENT CONFERENCES

Your attitudes toward performance improvement conferences will greatly determine your effectiveness in conducting them. Many of the negative attitudes sales managers and sales representatives have toward these conferences are the result of forced, uninformed evaluations and inept discussions of performance. As already pointed out, evaluations should be the result of field work-withs and should be based on clearly defined, mutually agreed on performance standards. A sales manager who is forced to make evaluations without knowledge of field performance fears the conference because he knows he'll be talking about a subject he knows too little about. A sales representative who is forced to face an evaluation with only a vague idea of performance criteria which is used to judge him looks on the conference as a foreboding experience. Most negative attitudes toward performance improvement conferences can be eliminated by thoughtful preparation and participative, improvement oriented conferences.

PRACTICE EXERCISE: Attitudes toward Performance
Improvement Conferences

Take time to examine your attitudes by answering the questions presented below:

WALKING IN

1. Think of your first performance improvement conference. What were you thinking and feeling when you walked in?

_____

2. Would you characterize the attitude of the last person you evaluated as resisting or open?

_____

3. What do you think your top sales representative will be thinking as he walks into his next conference?

_____

DURING THE CONFERENCE

1. How did you feel talking about yourself during your last conference?

_____

2. What is your biggest fear in conducting an improvement conference?

_____

3. What should be included in an improvement plan?

_____

FOLLOWING THE CONFERENCE

1. If you have a sincere interest in your sales representative's development, what type of follow-up is needed after the conference?

_____

2. What were the goals of your own improvement plan following your last conference?

_____

PREPARING FOR A PERFORMANCE IMPROVEMENT CONFERENCE

Successful improvement conferences do not happen by chance, they are the result of careful preparation. In preparing for a conference:

- *Inform the sales representative in advance.*
  Let the sales representative know in advance that you plan to hold a performance improvement conference and let him know the time and place it will be held.

- *Evaluate the sales representative and let him evaluate himself.*
  Complete the evaluation form yourself and ask the sales representative to evaluate himself using the same evaluation standards. This will give both you and the sales representative a chance to think through his performance and come prepared to discuss it.

- *Choose a suitable place and allow sufficient time.*
  Since you will be talking about personal performance, choose a place where you will not be interrupted and where you will not be overheard. Also, allow sufficient time. Allow the sales representative time to provide additional information and to discuss his performance, particularly if he is in disagreement.

- *Plan the conference.*
  You know how you would like the sales representative to change. You also know him as a person. As a result, you have some idea of the response to your evaluation. Use this knowledge to develop some questions to stimulate conversation during the conference.

THE ROLE OF DEVELOPER

Earlier, it was pointed out that sales representatives, like all people, resist change. It was also suggested that the key to bringing about change in a conference is *participation*. If the goal is development, the sales manager must adopt a role of developer and avoid the role of the know-it-all. The difference between the two roles is pointed out below:

Know-it-all role	Developer role
• Talks to • Points out improvement needs. • Gives the sales representative an improvement plan.	• Talks with • Discusses performance improvement needs. • Works out an improvement plan with the sales representative.

CONDUCTING A PERFORMANCE IMPROVEMENT CONFERENCE

The performance improvement conference should be a conversation between the sales representative and you. In order to have a conversation, both the sales representative and the sales manager must participate. The sales representative must participate in the discovery of the need to change and participate in the development of the plan to improve. Performance must be discussed but it need not be discussed in an accusatory tone. Ideally, the performance improvement conference should be a two-way conversation.

Use the Evaluation Form

If you have asked the sales representative to complete an evaluation of his performance and you have also completed an evaluation on him, you have the basis for a conversation. The structure of the performance evaluation form suggests that there are performance areas that should be discussed separately. The form itself will suggest some order for the discussion. In the performance evaluation form for the spice sales representative, the performance areas are presented in this order: Merchandising shelves, building floor displays, selling and planning. The sequence in which the performance areas are presented on the form suggest that this would be the order in which they should be discussed.

Ask Questions

An evaluation of a sales representative's performance gives you something to talk about. Having something to talk about is all right if you plan to lecture a sales representative; you need questions if you plan to have a discussion. The kind of questions you need to ask are the thought provoking kind not the kind of questions that stimulate defensiveness and arguments.

Let's say, for example, your evaluation of a sales representative indicates he needs to keep better books. One way to start the conversation would be to directly confront him with the deficiency. A much better way would be to ask, "Do you feel you have the information on each of your accounts to plan effective sales programs?" Another approach would be to ask specific questions about one of the sales representative's accounts. For example, "How is distribution for our line in Super-Sam's?" Questions stimulate discussion. Discussion creates participation; participation is essential if meaningful change is to occur.

Ask Before you Tell

In discussing each performance area, you should begin with a question about the performance area. The principle to be followed is: *Ask before you tell.* The sales representative's answer to your question will serve as the basis for your conversation. During the conversation you will have a chance to point out the strengths and improvement needs in the performance area. Be tactful yet clear when you are introducing the performance weaknesses and allow the sales representative to reply. Listen to what he has to say and then together develop a mutually acceptable statement of improvement need. If you and the sales representative have a difference of opinion about his performance, be willing to sell your opinion to him.

DEVELOPING AN IMPROVEMENT PLAN

Isolating performance improvement needs is one thing, developing an improvement plan to eliminate or reduce performance deficiencies is another. Some performance deficiencies are the result of lack of information—the proper procedure or the company policy was not understood. These are easy to eliminate. Other deficiencies require extensive effort.

Improvement plans should contain statements of the improvement goals as well as the methods to be used to reach these goals. Improving skill in selling shelf changes to chain stores is a clear statement of an improvement goal. Focusing on one account a week, preparing a before and after shelf sketch, and writing out the sales presentation before making it are examples of the methods to be used to reach this goal.

PRACTICE EXERCISE: Developing an Improvement Plan

Following your evaluation of Harold Norman, you conclude he is a great doer but not much of a planner. When he is in a store, he does everything that needs to be done. Unfortunately, this slows him down and at the end of the day; he has to rush through his store calls. He does not realize that some of the store managers are aware of his rushed calls at the end of the day.

Outline below some of the questions you would ask him to get the conference started.

_____

_____

_____

_____

_____

Let's say that mid-way through the conference Harold admits he needs to change but turns to you for assistance. Outline below a suggested improvement plan to make Harold Norman a better planner:

_____

_____

_____

_____

_____

SUMMARY: EVALUATION AND IMPROVEMENT

Because selling involves sales methods or strategies as well as sales goals, it is important for sales managers to be skilled in evaluating the performance and developing improvement plans. Performance improvement begins with a statement of what a sales representative should be doing and how he should be doing it; this is a performance-oriented job description. This type of job description includes performance areas which collectively represent success and competency in sales. As a result, it can be converted easily into a performance evaluation form by rating each performance area involved in the job. Evaluation should lead to improvement; and it does, providing the sales manager understands and overcomes resistance to change. The performance improvement conference is designed to create an atmosphere of change in which the sales manager assumes the role of developer and discusses performance and, with the sales representative, develops an improvement plan.

QUESTIONS THAT NEED ANSWERS

To be sure that you understand the ideas discussed in this chapter, answer the following questions.

1. Training and performance improvement:
   a) are the same.
   b) deal with teaching new things.
   c) are different.
   d) involve shaping behavior.

2. A performance-oriented job description:
   a) states what is to be done and how it is to be done.
   b) has to be developed by the personnel department.
   c) indicates the performance goals to be reached.
   d) includes compensation elements.

3. A rating of "good" on an evaluation form means the sales representative:
   a) meets objectively valid standards.
   b) is the number one person on the team.
   c) meets the sales manager's standards for good.
   d) should be considered for promotion.

4. Change:
   a) implies criticism.
   b) upsets the pattern.
   c) produces fear.
   d) all of these.

5. The role of the sales manager in the performance improvement conference should be:
   a) teacher.
   b) developer.
   c) expert.
   d) leader.

If you made the following choices, you should feel that the ideas discussed are yours: 1c, 2a ,3c, 4d, 5b.

Chapter 7

Planning Team Sales Activities

PANIC BUTTON OR TARGET

Planning is not a favorite topic with people in sales management. It is almost alien to the "do something, activist" tradition that creates the excitement that attracts people to sales. One time, early in my career as a sales trainer, I was having difficulty getting a session started on planning. A sympathetic, experienced sales manager realized my predicament and jumped to his feet, went directly to the instruction board and drew a series of circles with a dot in the middle.

He said, "Gentlemen, there are only two ways for a sales manager to look at this, it is either a target or a panic button." He went on to state that a sales manager has only two choices, he spends his time responding to panic buttons *or* he accepts the role as target director. As he put it, "Sales managers must decide what they are going to keep their eye on—targets or panic buttons." Sales managers must decide whether they are going to let situations control them or whether they are going to control situations.

He then turned to me and said, "I'll make the choice for the group. We want to be target directors and that means we want to be better planners." That statement permitted me to start the session on planning.

PLANNING DEFINED

Planning can be defined as the process of developing a proposed course of action. Planning consists of thinking through what you are going to do before you do it.

Planning Includes:
- Setting goals.
- Determining resources available.
- Deciding on methods to reach goals.
- Establishing schedules.

One example of a plan would be the plan for introducing a new product.

The Goals:	Distribution in 80 percent of the stores in the market. (2,000)
	Floor displays in 50 percent of the merchandisable stores. (400)
The Resources:	A sales team of 5 people and a manager.
	400 floor display cards.
	Sampling kit and product presentation folder.
	Newspaper ads.
The Methods:	Introductory sales meeting.
	Distribution and floor goal planning by each salesperson.
	Use of sample kit and product presentation folder in the sales presentation to retailers.
The Schedule:	*First week*—hold the introductory meeting and gain distribution goals in 1,000 accounts and floor displays in 100 accounts.

> *Second week*—gain distribution in 500 more accounts and floor displays in 140 additional accounts.
> *Third week*—gain distribution in all of the remaining accounts and floor displays in 60 additional accounts.
> *Fourth week*—gain floor displays in 100 additional accounts.

In this chapter on planning, four stages of planning will be examined, systems for planning programs, forecasting sales and scheduling time will be presented.

WHY SHOULD SALES MANAGERS PLAN?

A sales manager who plans gets more done and achieves better results, than one who plays it by ear. Normally, a sales manager who takes time to think through the goals he wants to reach and thinks through how and when he wants to reach them reaches more goals than a sales manager who just does things without thinking.

Sales managers should plan because they are required to reach a large number of goals in a limited time. Planning is the only way a sales manager can be sure of reaching *all* of the goals he has to reach. Without proper planning, it's almost a foredrawn conclusion that some goals just won't be reached. In addition, without a plan, a sales manager can not *measure progress* toward a goal. A plan also helps a sales manager think through the difficulties he'll have before they occur.

THE FIRST STEP IN PLANNING: SETTING GOALS

A plan is developed to accomplish a goal or objective. The first step in planning is to state the goal or objective in measurable terms. For example: five new placements per sales representative each day.

It should be obvious that some goals are better, more directional than others. The goal, "Getting more facings on the shelf" is less desirable than the goal, "getting one more facing on the shelf in 30 key accounts in a market." The first goal is not specific and is not measurable. "More" is not specific or measurable; "One and 30" are specific and measurable.

The goal, "100 percent distribution of all sizes of a product in all accounts" is less desirable than the goal, "50 percent distribution of three sizes of a product in key accounts." The first goal is pure blue sky; it is unattainable in most situations and not really compatible with all of the goals a sales team must reach in a market area. Every plan that we develop should have realistic goals. A *realistic goal* is a goal that can be attained within the limitations of existing conditions. A realistic goal is: specific, measurable, attainable and compatible.

A Realistic Goal is:

- Specific
- Measurable
- Attainable
- Compatible

A goal is *specific* if it is perfectly clear what the target is. There is no chance of misinterpretation. For example, the goal: "Better shelf promotion" is not specific. The goal: "Shelves with shelf strips for promoted products" is specific.

A goal is *measurable* if it can be counted or converted to a number. For example, the goal: "50 floor stackings" is measurable; the goal: "As many floor stackings as possible" is not measurable.

A goal is *attainable* if it can be reached within the limits of available resources. For example, the goal: "60 floor displays a month" is probably attainable. The goal: "200 floor displays in a territory in a month" is probably not attainable.

A goal is *compatible* if it can be reached without risking the other goals that must be reached within the same time period. For example, the goal of complete distribution of a new product in all accounts in a week is usually not compatible with normal account coverage. The goal could not be reached without sacrificing other essential goals. The goal: "Complete distribution of a new product in 15 accounts in a week" would be compatible.

Setting Priorities

Planning should permit us to reach many goals simultaneously. This is only possible if priorities are assigned to the goals. Setting priorities will insure that all essential goals will be reached.

> *Priority Setting* consists of determining which goals *must* be reached and which goals are *desirable* but not critical.

Priority setting can be accomplished by assigning each goal a number. The number indicates the order of importance and indicates the priority of importance of the goal.

PRACTICE EXERCISE: Priority Selling

Rate each of the sales activities in the order of importance as you see them by placing a number 1 next to activity you consider most important; a number 2 next to the one you consider next most important, etc.

For example: If you consider (9) Administrative Work your number 1 priority—place a number 1 to the right of that activity.

List of Activities: Third Week of the Month   *Priority*

1. Work with Betty Williams, new sales representative, her first week on the job.   _____
2. Work with Tom Jones. He's sold only 25 percent of his displays, and 2/3 of the time period is gone.   _____
3. Work with Bruce Andrews: poor distribution on large sizes. Good performance on selling floors.   _____
4. Call on chain headquarters to introduce new product and present next month's programs.   _____
5. Conduct sales meeting. Review current program performance prior to the final week's push. Introduce next month's program.   _____
6. Survey Bill St. John's territory. He is your best sales representative and is doing well on all current programs, but it has been six months since you worked with Bill and two months since you surveyed his territory.   _____
7. Find out how the new package of a competitive product is selling.   _____
8. Work with older sales representative—Harold Hansen's total sales are trending downward.   _____
9. Administrative Work: Catch up on paperwork.   _____

THE SECOND STEP IN PLANNING: DETERMINING RESOURCES AVAILABLE

When and how a goal is reached is very much influenced by the resources available. Resources are the people, money and the material available to reach those goals. Since resources are usually limited, goals must be viewed in terms of the resources available to reach them. Obviously, a sales force selling 30 products with each sales representative assigned 50 accounts has more resources available than a sales force selling 60 products with sales representatives covering 100 accounts. A plan developed without a clear awareness of resources available seldom is successful.

All plans are based on a determination of the resources available. Sometimes the determination is carefully made; sometimes not. In developing a plan that you hope will be effective, it is important to determine the skills of the people involved, the quantity of materials available, and the specific equipment that is needed. If you develop a plan based on the assumption that you will have resources that are not really available to you, your plan will fail in terms of time, resources and results. Therefore, when you develop a plan, be sure that the resources you planned on having are actually available. Modify the plan whenever resource availability changes.

THE THIRD STEP IN PLANNING: DECIDING ON A METHOD

Goals have been set. Resources have been evaluated. It is now time to determine the *method* to be used to reach the goals with the available resources. *Method consists of the things that must be done to reach a goal.*

While there is usually more than one way to reach a goal, not all methods are equally successful. For example, a sales manager might have a telephone conversation with one of his sales representatives and tell him to sell more floor displays or he could work with him in the field and show him how to sell more floor displays. Both methods are designed to help the sales representative sell floor displays but the work-with will probably help the sales representative sell more displays.

.Sales managers have three things to consider at this stage in planning.

- Consider more than one method of reaching a goal.
- Determine the limitations that resources impose on methods.
- Decide on the best method to use.

Consider More Than One Method

Since there are always a number of ways or methods that can be used to reach a goal, more than one method or technique should be considered in developing a plan. Sales managers are frequently *too ready to choose the first method* that comes to mind. One of the real tests of planning skill is the ability to come up with more than one method of reaching a goal.

In searching for alternative methods from which to choose, ask, "What are the various ways that can be used to reach the goal." Don't be satisfied with one or two methods. There are usually many methods available and you just have to take the time to think of them.

The three recommendations that can be made to develop alternative methods are:

- Go beyond easy methods.
- Think creatively yourself.
- Use other people—brainstorm.

The basic point we are trying to make is that when you have a variety of methods to choose from, you have a better chance of choosing a good one. Keep thinking—consider as many methods as time permits.

Developing Alternate Methods

Methods may be developed as the result of past or current experiences or they may be developed by use of one's personal creative powers. The first type of planner is called the *resourceful* strategist. The second type of planner is called the *creative* strategist.

The *resourceful strategist* uses his knowledge of similar situations and develops strategies based on this knowledge. Skill in resourcefulness can best be developed by looking for similarities in situations and studying methods used by others.

The *creative strategist* uses his ingenuity and imagination to develop new strategies. While some people seem to be naturally more creative than others, all of us can be much more creative than we think we are. The big obstacle to creativity is fear of being different. Once we have overcome this fear, our creative powers can more easily be utilized.

Brainstorming Technique

Developing novel and imaginative strategies is a big problem in the advertising business. The brainstorming technique has proved to be one of the best techniques for developing novel and imaginative ideas.

The brainstorming technique differs from standard planning in two ways:

1. All suggestions are welcome—no matter how far out, anything goes.
2. No one is allowed to criticize, censure or evaluate any of the suggestions offered.

The result: People stimulate people; ideas stimulate ideas.

A way-out suggestion leads to a more practical solution. Fear of expressing new and different ideas is reduced. New and different ideas flow more steadily.

Try the brainstorming technique the next time you have a particularly difficult goal to reach and need a creative solution.

Determine the Limitation That Resources Impose on Methods

Once a number of ways have been developed, each method must be evaluated by determining the likelihood of reaching the goal within the limits of the available resources. For example:

Method #1
Sell retailers in the store   Goal:
————————————————————▶ Open Account

Method #2
Sell retailers at lunch   Goal:
————————————————————▶ Open Account

The first method will lead to the goal—the second requires lunch money (a resource that is not available).

THE FOURTH STEP: DEVELOP A SCHEDULE

The dream "I want to be a millionaire" is a dream to most of us because we have no method for reaching the goal and in addition it is a dream because it lacks a time frame. There is no schedule for becoming a millionaire.

A plan without a schedule is no plan at all. A plan must include a completion time for final goals as well as sub-goals. To plan the goal: "Gain distribution in 30 new accounts for large sizes of your product" is not a plan unless it is assigned a time frame; *"30 new accounts in 30 days" makes it a plan.* An even better plan has time frames for sub-goals.

- 10 new accounts in the first week.
- 10 new accounts in the second week.
- 5 new accounts in the third week.
- 5 new accounts in the fourth week.

It is a better plan because each sub-goal has been assigned a time frame and progress toward the final goals can be tracked. The major benefit of scheduling is that it provides a way of measuring progress. There are no surprises at the end of the time period. If sub-goals are not reached on time, something can be done before it is too late.

While there are many factors that can affect your week-by-week goals, it is generally accepted that during the early part of a plan, a substantially higher percent of the goals reached should be scheduled than percent of time elapsed.

Most plans should be scheduled so that:
- *40 percent of the goals* can be reached by the end of first week.
- *60 percent of the goals* can be reached by end of second week.
- *85 percent of the goals* can be reached by end of third week.
- *100 percent of the goals* can be reached by end of fourth week.

PLANNING WORKSHEET

A planning worksheet is presented on the following page. Use the planning worksheet and your planning skills will increase.

PLANNING WORKSHEET

(1)   THE GOAL: _____

_____

(2)   THE RESOURCES: _____

_____

_____

(3)   THE METHOD: _____

_____

_____

_____

_____

_____

(4)   THE SCHEDULE: _____

_____

Criteria for Evaluating a Plan

- Does the plan have SMAC?
- Have the resources been evaluated accurately?
- Are the methods clearly indicated?
- Has a schedule been developed to check progress?
- Can the plan be modified if conditions change?

Criteria for Evaluating a Plan

Our discussion of planning suggests that criteria could be developed for evaluating plans. The chart presented below suggests such criteria:

Criteria for Evaluating the Effectiveness of a Plan

- Does this plan have specific, measurable, attainable, compatible goals?
- Have the available resources been accurately evaluated?
- Are the things to be done to reach the goals clearly indicated?
- Has a time schedule been developed for completing each activity?
- Can the plan be varied and modified if conditions change?

These criteria have been included on the planning worksheet.

PRACTICE EXERCISE: Evaluating a Plan

Using the planning worksheet presented below, evaluate the sales manager's plan for helping Guy sell an additional 100 cases during the month of August.

PLANNING WORKSHEET

(1)   THE GOAL: Help Guy sell an additional 100 cases during the month of August.

(2)   THE RESOURCES: Commission on cases sold, two days of your time. 20 days of Guy's time, 100 accounts, retailers' rapport with Guy.

(3)   THE METHOD: Sit down with Guy—help him think through where additional cases can be sold. Suggest that he sell 40 cases of expensive cases to his 2 major accounts. 50 cases of low priced product to 2 accounts which do catering and 10 cases to 2 key summer accounts. Talk through the 3 sales pitches needed and work with him in making the pitches to the caterers.

(4)   THE SCHEDULE: Monday, August 4th, Meet with Guy, set objectives, develop pitches.

Week of 4th—Sell major accounts.

August 12th—Work with Guy in selling caterers.

Week of 18th—Sell summer accounts.

YOUR EVALUATION OF THE PLAN: _____

_____

_____

PLANNING A PRODUCT PROGRAM

The purpose of programming is to get a sales representative to give one or a group of products concentrated attention. Through programming, you give one or more of your products top priority for a period of time. During this time, usually a month or a week, sales representatives focus their attention on the sales and merchandising of the programmed products. Program objectives of necessity are store level objectives. Program goals usually involve selling retailers merchandising ideas such as floor stacks, new shelf facings or new distribution.

Program Planning Sequence

A suggested sequence for planning a product program or promotion is presented on the chart on the following page.

PROGRAM PLANNING SEQUENCE

1. The Beginning

- Establish minimum goals and obtain support information

↓

2. Plan the Introduction

- Plan meeting
- Check support materials

↓

3. Conduct Meeting

- Announce and sell program
- Describe support material (advertising, POS, pricing)
- Discuss sales and merchandising strategy
- Give minimum goals

↓

4. Plan for Each Account (Pre-Plan)

- Review minimum goals
- Give sales representatives pre-plan forms
- Ask sales representatives to set program goals for each account

↓

5. Collect Pre-Plan Forms

- Collect each sales representatives completed pre-plan for each account
- Check and review to see that minimum goals have been met by each sales representative
- Review sales representatives' activities in key accounts
- Place a copy of each sales representatives' program pre-plan form in field fact book
- Pass out activity report forms for recording progress

↓

6. Launch the Program

- Give each sales representative his allocation of POS
- Hand out sales/pricing sheets if available

↓

7. Daily Follow-Up

- Review daily reports to spot sales representatives having difficulty selling program
- Work with sales representatives having difficulty
- Survey to verify reported program accomplishments

↓

8. Weekly Recap and Follow-Up

- Recap program results reported on daily reports at the end of the week
- Spot sales representatives not meeting goals and review pre-plan form with them

Our Weekly Goal Objectives:

40%	1st Week
60%	2nd Week
85%	3rd Week
100%	4th Week

- Determine accounts where sales representative is having problems and develop a new plan with him to sell the program to these accounts
- Work with sales representative if necessary

↓

SUCCESSFUL PROGRAM

PRE-PLANNING

An important part of the proposed program planning system is pre-planning. Pre-planning is a system for planning monthly or weekly programs which requires the sales representative to do four things: (1) Set specific program goals for each store. (2) Set the program goals himself. (3) Set the program goals before the program begins. (4) Write down the program goals set for each store. The pre-plan system has the advantage of specific, measurable goals and because the sales representative sets the goals himself, the goals are more likely to be attainable and compatible.

The biggest objection to pre-planning is that it takes time. Admittedly, it takes time but the question is, is it time well spent? The time required at the sales meeting to pre-plan programs can usually be found without an undue burden on sales representatives. The pre-plan then becomes an organizing force in the sales representative's daily activities and makes him a more efficient, productive person.

The Benefits of Pre-Planning

Pre-planning gives the sales representative an opportunity to review business opportunities in each store in his territory. Because he sets his own goals, he is more inclined to do his best to reach them. Setting goals ahead of time helps the sales representative to target his activities. Writing down the goals to be reached in each store allows him to track his progress and isolate the stores in which he is having difficulty.

As a manager, pre-planning allows you to track progress toward attainment of team goals and focuses your efforts when problems develop. Written pre-plans let you know where the sales representatives plan to reach their sales and merchandising goals and allow you to evaluate the attainability of the goals which are set.

Procedure for Pre-Planning Programs

Each sales representative should:

- Determine the goals that will be met in his *territory*.
  A. The minimum floor and shelf goals are usually given to him for merchandisable accounts.

   B. He must determine if he can set higher floor merchandising goals for these accounts.

- Using knowledge of the accounts, decide what goals can be reached in *each account*. List the goals on a pre-plan form.
- Review the goals for each account before each call and report goals that are reached and those that are not.

The Pre-Plan Form

The pre-plan form consists of a column for listing the account names and four sets of columns for each week of the month. The weekly columns are subdivided into columns for four different program goals.

PRE-PLAN FORM

SALES REPRESENTATIVE _____

TERRITORY _____

DAY: M T W TH F

Account Name & Address	1st Week (40%)	2nd Week (60%)	3rd Week (85%)	4th Week (100%)

The purpose of this form is to give the sales representative a place to list the program goals he plans to reach in each account each week of the month. The sales representative then reviews the goals daily and circles goals as they are met.

PRACTICE EXERCISE: Pre-Planning Program Goals for an Account

Assume that you are the sales representative calling on Corner Cove Delicatessen. Examine the sales and merchandising information presented below and then set program goals for Corner Cove for this month's program. The programmed product is pink olives.

CORNER COVE DELICATESSEN

Case Sales History

Pink Olives

	January	February	March	April	May	June
Small jar	2 1 3 2	1 3 5 2				
Medium jar	3 3 2 3	3 2 2 2				
Large jar	1 3 1 6	3 3 3 2				

Shelf Position: Because the retailer considers them a novelty item, he has so far resisted efforts to find space for them in the olive section.

Floor Merchandising: The retailer has ample space for floor merchandising but so far he has not displayed pink olives. He generally puts high-priced goods on the floor.

This month you have advertising support and a special tie-in case card. List the program goals you would set for Corner Cove Delicatessen.

PRE-PLAN FORM

Account Name & Address	1st Week (40%)	2nd Week (60%)	3rd Week (85%)	4th Week (100%)
1. Corner Cove				

FORECASTING CASE SALES

An important part of every monthly program is the estimate made of the case sales that can be produced by the type of sales activity that programming produces. These estimates are actually forecasts of future sales. Your involvement in estimating or forecasting case sales is not limited to programming; annual budgets and case sales predictions for production are also part of your job.

A sales forecast is nothing more than an estimate of future sales. In order to forecast, you must have some knowledge of past performance of the product in your market, an awareness of current market conditions and some idea of anticipated future conditions. If conditions affecting sales in the past and present do not change, future sales will be the same as past sales. For example: If you sold 2,300 cases in January of last year, you should expect to sell 2,300 cases in January of this year, if conditions remain the same. If conditions affecting sales in the past are different from those that you anticipate will exist in the future, future sales will be different. For example: If you sold 2,300 cases in January of last year with the support of heavy advertising and no advertising is planned for January of this year, you most likely will not sell 2,300 cases this year. Sales forecasting requires you to know as completely as possible the conditions affecting sales that existed in the past and to anticipate or make predictions of the conditions affecting sales that will exist in the future.

Conditions Affecting Forecasts

Some of the conditions that seem to affect future case sales have been listed below. In making forecasts of future case sales, look for changes in these conditions and adjust your estimates accordingly.

1. *Seasonal Fluctuations:* Sales of some products increase during the summer months and others decrease. Sales of other products may increase during the Christmas and Easter seasons.
2. *Going into or from a Program:* Generally, sales of a product will increase during the month it is featured on a program and level off or decrease the month following the program.

3. *Program Content:* A program supported with advertising will tend to produce more sales than a program not supported by advertising.

4. *Trends in the Type of Product Sold:* Sales of one type of product may be on the increase while sales of another type of product may be holding steady.

5. *New Products:* The introduction of a new product usually affects the sales of similar products. It may decrease sales of similar products, or it may help to increase the sales of these products.

6. *Price Changes:* Whenever price increases are announced, sales tend to increase in the month before the increase takes place.

7. *Package Changes:* In almost all instances when there is a package change, sales of a product will change. Usually they increase, sometimes they decrease.

8. *Sales Coverage:* Changes in the field sales organization usually produce changes in sales. A new sales representative in a territory or an increase in the number of accounts can produce decreases.

PRACTICE EXERCISE: Cookie Program

Traditionally, each June your team has a cookie program. Every year in the past, the program has included radio advertising and extensive in-store sales promotion work. Banners, floor displays, sampling programs, shelf displays were all used to back the program. This year both television and radio will be used but there will be a cut back in-store sales promotion. Only floor display cards will be available. Another change that has occurred is that there is one less sales representative on the team.

Using the information presented below, make case sales forecast and floor display forecast for the team and list them in the appropriate column.

Sales Person	Accounts Assigned	Sales– June Previous Year	Sales– May This Year	Forecast– June This Year	Displays Last Year	Forecast Displays This Year
Jackson	40	250	100		40	
Anderson	35	110	90		5	
Travolta	45	300	155		35	
Schilling	48	282	134		38	

What information would you like to have had in making this forecast that you did not have? _____

_____

_____

_____

PLANNING YOUR OWN SCHEDULE

So much for forecasting and planning programs. Now it is time to consider how you should plan for yourself. Planning for yourself involves deciding on the goals you want to reach, setting priorities and developing a schedule to reach the goals you set.

In our earlier discussion of planning it was pointed out that unless activities required to reach goals are scheduled, they will not be reached. Or, to put it another way, unless you allocated your time to the really important activities, you will end up at month's end with too few goals met.

While your intentions may be good, the demands on your time make it essential that your time be scheduled in advance. More than one sales manager has failed because he took care of pressing demands, accepted excuses for not working the field and ended up getting very little accomplished.

Scheduling and Time Management

Almost all approaches to time management require you to keep a record of how you currently schedule your time. These records are then used to make the point: Some of the things you do are not essential to your success. A critical examination of your own time utilization would probably yield the same conclusion: some of your time could be better spent.

SYSTEM FOR SCHEDULING YOUR TIME

A more positive approach to time management is to take time out at the end of each month and each week and decide on the goals you want to reach in the coming month or week. Once the goals have been stated, determine the things you have to do to reach these goals and schedule your time accordingly. A more detailed explanation of this monthly and weekly scheduling system is presented on the next page:

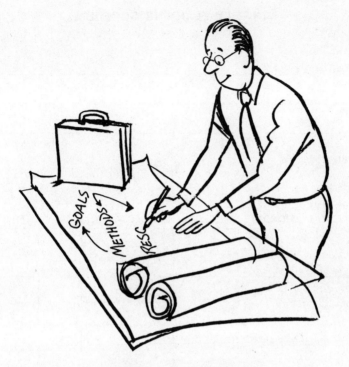

The Monthly Planning Schedule

At the end of the month:
1. List all of the goals you want to reach in the coming month.
2. Decide on the things you must do to reach these goals.
3. Plot these activities on a monthly planning schedule.

The monthly planning schedule gives you a place to list all of the goals you want to reach and gives you space for plotting your activities on a day-by-day basis.

While the monthly planning schedule takes time to complete, it has proved to be immensely effective in directing activities and in helping sales managers reach their goals. The monthly planning schedule commits you to a specific activity of special importance each day. At the same time, it is flexible enough to permit change if necessary.

A monthly planning schedule is presented on the following page.

MONTHLY PLANNING SCHEDULE

This Month's Goals: _____

_____

_____

Activity Schedule

SATURDAY/ SUNDAY	MONDAY	TUESDAY	WEDNESDAY	THURSDAY	FRIDAY

The Weekly Planning Schedule

At the end of the week:
1. Recap the goals you reached and determine those you still need to reach.
2. Review monthly planning list activities for the following week and also list important goals not met the previous week.
3. Develop a detailed weekly schedule for the following week based on this list of activities and goals.
4. Make necessary appointments and schedule sales representatives' work-withs.

The weekly planning schedule is nothing but an extension of the monthly planning schedule. Changes have to be made to monthly plans because of unanticipated developments. The weekly planning schedule can be even more specific than the monthly schedule. There are fewer unknowns. Attainment of short term goals is more pressing. The weekly planning schedule should be on your boss's desk Friday afternoon prior to the week planned.

A weekly planning schedule is presented on the next page:

SALES MANAGER'S WEEKLY SCHEDULE

SALES MANAGER ROGER GRAND WEEK ENDING JUNE 16

DAY	ACTIVITY		REASON	RESULTS
Monday 12	A.M.	SURVEY LUCIFER THOMAS' TERRITORY		
	P.M.			
Tuesday 13	A.M.	WORK-WITH LUCIFER THOMAS IN TERRITORY		
	P.M.	SURVEY REPORTED SHELF SETS IN MARTIN BRUCES' TERRITORY		
Wednesday 14	A.M.	WORK WITH GEORGE DAVID IN TERRITORY		
	P.M.	LEAVE FIELD 4 P.M. WEDDING ANNIVERSARY		
Thursday 15	A.M.	WORK WITH RONALD LOPER IN TERRITORY		
	P.M.			
Friday 16	A.M.	OFFICE ADMINISTRATION		
	P.M.	HEADQUARTERS CALL JERRY'S CHAIN STORE		

PRACTICE EXERCISE: Roger Grand's Weekly Schedule

Roger Grand is a sales manager of a team responsible for selling jelly, peanut butter and crackers. The monthly program goals and the first week results are shown in the recap presented below. Review the weekly recap and on the basis of the recap, make recommendations for changing Roger Grand's schedule.

WEEKLY RECAP OF SALES AND MERCHANDISING OBJECTIVES

End of the first week—June 9th

| | FLOOR DISPLAY | | | SHELF | |
	APPLE JELLY	PEANUT BUTTER	CRACKERS	IN CRACKER SECTION	NEW JELLY SET
GEORGE DAVID					
Total # accts.	31	31	31	31	31
Reached 1st week	5	7	6	6	12
Goals for month	(17)	(25)	(22)	(15)	(15)
MARTIN BRUCE					
Total # accts.	33	33	33	33	33
Reached 1st week	7	21	12	13	21
Goals for month	(29)	(25)	(22)	(16)	(16)
LARRY BAUER					
Total # accts.	37	37	37	37	37
Reached 1st week	20	19	15	8	14
Goals for month	(31)	(30)	(26)	(18)	(18)
LUCIFER THOMAS					
Total # accts.	40	40	40	40	40
Reached 1st week	10	15	10	6	18
Goals for month	(34)	(32)	(28)	(20)	(20)
RONALD LOPER					
Total # accts.	37	37	37	37	37
Reached 1st week	6	2	9	6	29
Goals for month	(31)	(30)	(26)	(18)	(18)

SALES MANAGER'S WEEKLY SCHEDULE

SALES MANAGER _____ WEEK ENDING _____

DAY	ACTIVITY	REASON	RESULTS
Monday	A.M.		
	P.M.		
Tuesday	A.M.		
	P.M.		
Wednesday	A.M.		
	P.M.		
Thursday	A.M.		
	P.M.		
Friday	A.M.		
	P.M.		

FIELD FACT BOOK

In order to plan, a sales manager needs *information*. While some planning can be done in the office, many important plans are developed in the field. Consequently, some thought should be given as to what *information* you need to take with you into the field.

What information do you need to have at your fingertips in order to develop result-oriented plans? While some sales managers would list almost every record they have, experience has shown that the most frequently used pieces of information are:

1. **Goals and Schedules**
   a. Your current monthly and weekly schedule.
   b. List of monthly program goals by territory.
2. **Team Information**
   a. Roster: name/address, telephone number of salespersons.
   b. List of accounts by territory.
3. **Territory Information**
   a. Personal information on the sales representative assigned to the territory.
   b. Performance evaluations and improvement plans for the sales representative.
   c. Copies of memos to the sales representative.
   d. Program planning sheets for the month.
   e. Daily reports for the most current week.
   f. The account coverage schedule for the territory.
   g. An account profile for the territory.
   h. Distribution by account for the territory.

The recommended system for having this information available in the field is to develop and carry with you a field fact book. The field fact book is a three-ring binder, usually 3 inches thick. It should be divided into three major sections:

- Goals and schedules
- Team information
- Territory information

SUMMARY: THE BEST LAID PLANS OF MEN

There is an element of chance in every plan that you develop. Even the best laid plans of men fail. But the people who act without a plan fail more frequently than those with a plan.

This chapter was designed to help you learn to plan for your team. Setting measurable goals, determining the resources available, deciding on methods, and establishing specific and realistic schedules are all a part of this. Learning to handle these all-important managerial responsibilities will help you become a more skillful manager.

QUESTIONS THAT NEED ANSWERS

To be sure that you understand the ideas discussed in this chapter, answer the following questions:

1. Planning can be defined as:
   a) setting goals and deciding on methods to reach them.
   b) determining resources available.
   c) establishing deadlines.
   d) all of these.

2. Your goals should always be:
   a) vague and general.
   b) flexible and modest.
   c) specific and measurable.
   d) developed with additional equipment and personnel in mind.

3. In developing a plan, be sure that your resources are:
   a) comparable to your competition's.
   b) actually available.
   c) designed to push you and your sales representatives to the limit.
   d) within financial limits.

4. Pre-planning is a method of planning:
   a) at territory level.
   b) at account level.
   c) at team level.
   d) all of these.

5. Programs:
   a) focus attention.
   b) liven up a sales meeting.
   c) are simply schedules.
   d) result in reward.

6. Forecasts are nothing more than:
    a) guesses.
    b) estimates of future sales.
    c) predictions based on the past.
    d) blue sky optimism.

7. Brainstorming is a technique for developing:
    a) alternative goals.
    b) realistic decisions.
    c) creative strategies.
    d) practical schedules.

8. Time management:
    a) suggests ways of finding time.
    b) eliminates paperwork.
    c) is your own business.
    d) means you make better use of your time.

9. According to the recommended schedule, by the end of the second week
    a) 50 percent of the goals should be reached.
    b) 60 percent of the goals should be reached.
    c) 70 percent of the goals should be reached.
    d) 40 percent of the goals should be reached.

10. The field fact book lets a manager:
    a) know who to collect from.
    b) keep survey notes.
    c) plan in the field.
    d) all of these.

If you made the following choices, you should feel that the ideas discussed are yours: 1a, 2c, 3b, 4b, 5a, 6b, 7c, 8d, 9b, 10c.

Chapter 8

Controlling Sales Activity

IF YOU PULL A STRING, SOMETHING SHOULD HAPPEN

One of the reasons sales managers exist is that there is a pervading idea in business that it is possible to know what is going on in the field on a sales team and it is possible to do something to control this sales activity. This is not to say that a sales manager is a puppeteer who pulls the strings and sales representatives dance; it is to say that he should know what his people are doing and if they need to be re-directed he can do it. The companies that believe it is possible to control sales activities do not ask a sales manager to cover a territory or be responsible for key accounts. They know that controlling the activities of a sales team is a full-time job.

PLANNING AND CONTROL

Planning and control are interconnected management skills. A good plan includes a schedule and control consists of following up on the scheduled activities. A simple definition of planning is: *The process of thinking through what you are going to do before you do it.* Control is defined as *the process of seeing that what you want to get done actually gets done.*

THE CONTROL PROCESS

Control is a word used to describe the things you do to keep on top of team sales activity. At all times, you should know which sales goals and merchandising objectives are being met and which are not being met. When it is discovered that a planned sales goal or specified merchandising objective is not being met, a problem exists and a solution must be found.

Control consists of:
- Measuring
- Evaluating
- Directing

Measuring is the process of obtaining information about sales goals and merchandising objectives. The accuracy and timeliness of the information you have will determine to a great extent the effectiveness of the control you have over field sales activity.

Once information has been obtained, it must be *evaluated* for meaning. Knowing, for example, that the sales representatives are having difficulty selling shelf position for a new product is a piece of information. This information must be evaluated before it can be useful in directing sales activity. Are all of the sales representatives having difficulty or just some of them? What objections are being raised to the suggested shelf position for the new product?

Evaluation really consists of defining the cause of the problem.

The last step in the control process is to *direct* the activities of the sales representatives. If everything is happening as planned, no additional or different direction needs to be given. If a problem has been spotted, a solution has to be developed. Whatever the problem, you must develop a solution or your sales and merchandising goals will not be reached.

Control consists of measuring, evaluating and directing the activities of the members of your sales team. In this chapter we will discuss the information needed for the sales control function, define a process for evaluating information and suggest ways of directing the activities of sales team members.

MEASURING

The three sources of information needed to control field sales activity are:

- Sales representatives' activity reports
- Field survey observations
- Company and industry records

Sales representatives' activity reports give you information on the account coverage: accounts called on and what was accomplished. Your own field observations give you information on the conditions of your products in the stores. Company records like computer printouts give you a picture of case sales or shipments. Industry reports give you a basis of comparing your results with industry results.

Sales Representatives' Activity Report

Daily or weekly activity reports are used by almost all sales organizations to control the sales activity of their sales representatives. Ideally, the activity report is the sales representative's report to his boss, the sales manager, on what he was able to accomplish in the time period reported. The report indicates the accounts that were called on and what was accomplished on each call. The accomplishments include not only case sales but also shelf and floor activity.

Activity reports contain the information a sales manager needs to direct the activities of his salespeople. Without the kind of current information the activity report provides, it is impossible for a sales manager to do much about sales and merchandising objectives until it is too late. The end of the promotion report is history; the daily or weekly activity report is a report of ongoing efforts. The sales representative indicates where he is having difficulty and where he is succeeding. If read when received, it can be reviewed and help provided before the promotion or program is over.

The question of frequency of activity reports is best answered by you. When do you plan to use them? Daily or weekly? If you don't plan to read them every day, don't ask for them every day. If you plan to use them at the end of the week, ask for a weekly report.

As previously pointed out, the activity report should contain only the information you plan to use. It should also contain information not obtainable elsewhere and it should be as easy to complete as possible. Simple checkmarks and number entries are preferred.

PRACTICE EXERCISE: Evaluating an Activity Report

Evaluate Rudy Burns's daily activity report by answering the questions.

DAILY ACTIVITY REPORT

Name: Rudy Burns   Territory: #856   Day Friday   Date 22 August
Promotion: Small size, red and white.

Account Address	Account Class.	Retailer's Name	Sales Goals Reached Brand/Size	Merchandising Goals Reached Shelf	Merchandising Goals Reached Floor
Jewel #2			White/small-2cs Red/large&small-20cs	—	No!
NATCO			White/small-2cs Red/large&small-2cs	Moved Product	Bad Location, but on floor.
Deli Dan's			White/small-10cs Red/large-12cs	POS	No room
Jewel #3			White/small-2cs Red/small-1cs	—	No.
Eric's			No distribution of small sizes, 1 case red & white large.		

Comments: In addition to my concentrated efforts to push the program for small sizes of red and white, I sold 100 cases of other products. This program looks like a loser; I can't seem to get the floors for the product even though they are authorized in chain accounts. The stuff tastes terrible; I know it and the managers know it.

Do you feel this report gives you a picture of Rudy Burns's sales activities?

What information would you eliminate or add?

What would you do to direct the activities of sales representative Rudy Burns if you have received the daily activity report presented above?

DESIGNING FORMS AND REPORTS TO OBTAIN INFORMATION

Designing forms for other people to complete is an easy matter if you don't mind how you inconvenience them and don't have to rely on the reliability of the information provided. Every salesperson has used a form or report which seemed unduly complicated or really unnecessary. Because this type of form or report exists, it might be well to examine the forms or reports currently in use on your sales team. In evaluating these forms or reports, these questions should be asked:

- What information is obtained from the form or report?
- Do you use this information?
- Can this information be obtained more reliably or more quickly from another source?
- Is the form easy to complete?
- Is the time deadline for submitting the report necessary?

If the information obtained from the form or report is either not used or more reliably or more quickly obtained from another source, the report or form is unessential and should be eliminated. Sometimes, some of the information on a form is being used and other information is not being used. In this instance, the form should be revised to eliminate all unused information. If the form or report provides useful information not obtainable in the same time frame elsewhere, then it should be retained and the ease of completion examined. Some forms ask for a paragraph when a few words are all that is needed. Crisp, coded notations will give you some information much better than wordy descriptions. Reports which are of necessity detailed and comprehensive must allow ample room to present this type of information. Deadlines for completing reports and forms should be realistic and not set unless the information requested is needed by the deadline indicated. Asking for a report at the end of the day or within two days when it will not be used until the end of the week seldom makes sense. The considerations that must be made in evaluating a form are: the usefulness and timeliness of the information obtained.

FIELD OBSERVATIONS

The second source of information about sales and merchandising goals is field observations. Sales managers get a picture of in-store conditions when they work with sales representatives but they also can observe in-store conditions working without a sales representative.

Observing In-Store Conditions on Work-Withs

A great deal has already been said about the training and developing of sales representatives on work-withs. A work-with also permits you to observe and evaluate in-store accomplishments. Obviously, when a sales manager spots a problem on a work-with, it can be solved on the spot. For this reason, many sales managers feel that work-withs are the best way to make field observations. From a training and development point of view, they are correct. Unfortunately, there is one limitation on work-withs—the number of stores that can be observed in a day is restricted to the sales representative's call schedule. For this reason, it is recommended that sales managers spend some of their time surveying in-store conditions on their own.

Surveying In-Store Conditions

In merchandising oriented sales organizations like consumer product companies, there are few better ways of knowing what is going on than to observe conditions in retail stores. You can see for yourself how retailers are presenting your products to consumers.

Surveying can be defined as the process of observing in-store conditions of a representative number of stores in a market. The skills in surveying include:

- Choosing representative stores.
- Knowing what to notice.
- Organizing the call.

CHOOSING A REPRESENTATIVE SAMPLE OF STORES

Since the purpose of surveying is to observe conditions in stores and make generalizations about how your products are being presented to consumers, some thought should be given as to which stores are surveyed. Unless you choose representative stores, you will not get a *true picture* of in-store conditions in the marketing area. Since you can not usually observe every store in a marketing area, representative stores have to be chosen and inferences made about all of the stores.

For example, you sell through 300 retail stores. You have two hours in which to survey. Since it is impossible to visit all 300 stores in the two hours available, you must decide which stores to survey.

The method of selecting stores to be surveyed can be as casual as picking stores as you ride along a street, or as calculated as making a random selection of stores from a complete list of stores. While either way is acceptable to most salespeople, the stores you choose to survey must be representative of all of the stores.

The Ride and Plan Method

In this survey method, you select the streets and choose the stores on the streets to survey as you ride. Your knowledge of the marketing area determines the validity of the route and stores you choose. The purpose of the survey should determine which stores you observe. For example, every store should be observed if your purpose is to observe general market conditions, while only floor display accounts should be called on if your purpose is to observe floor display accomplishments.

The List and Map Method

The second survey method requires that a list of all the stores in a marketing area be available. Stores are chosen from the list and a route mapped to call on the stores. The key decision in this method is to determine which stores are representative. One way is to randomly select the stores. Random selection requires that: (1) each store on the list has the same chance of being chosen, (2) the choice of one store does not force the selection of another store. An example of the random selection of stores is to choose every fifth store on the list. The random selection method gives the best chance of a representative sample.

Another way to choose from a list is to survey all of the stores on the list in a part of the marketing area. An example of this way is to survey all of the stores in the northwest part of the market. One advantage of the list and map method eliminates the chance of missing an account as sometimes happens in the ride and pick method.

KNOWING WHAT TO NOTICE

The information you obtain in making in-store surveys is greatly influenced by what you are looking for. Distribution, case sales, shelf space and arrangement and floor and store promotions are the focus of most surveys made by consumer product sales managers. Information about these merchandising goals is hard to obtain elsewhere. Occasionally, retailer attitudes are the focus.

ORGANIZING THE SURVEY CALL

In order to increase the accuracy of observations and to maximize the information obtained, most sales managers find that an organized approach to making a call on a store is necessary. The seven-step call procedure presented below is an example of an organized call procedure used in one sales organization.

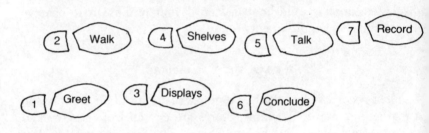

Step 1—Greet the retailer
Step 2—Walk the store
Step 3—Look at the floor displays
Step 4—Evaluate the shelves
Step 5—Talk with the retailer
Step 6—Reach conclusions
Step 7—Record your observations and conclusions

Step 1—Greet the Retailer

Introduce yourself and ask permission to survey the store. Try to delay the conversation with the retailer until after you survey the store. His comments about your products will make more sense after you have seen his store.

Step 2—Walk the Store

In order to get an overall impression of the store and to determine the retailer's shelf management and merchandising attitudes, walk through the whole store, not just the department in which your products are located.

Step 3—Look at the Floor Displays

Because floor displays are such an important part of building and maintaining the sales of a consumer product, most sales managers focus first on floor displays when they survey in-store conditions. Location, size, type of sign used and the number of products in a display area are some of the observations that should be recorded.

Step 4—Evaluate the Shelves

Space, location and arrangement of products are the focus of the shelf observations. Special shelf promotions including point of sale are also worthy of note.

Step 5—Talk with the Retailer

If the purpose of the survey requires you to get information from the retailer, take a few minutes to talk with the retailer before leaving the store. Competitive activity, buying trends and customer attitudes are examples of purposes that require talking with retailers.

Step 6—Reach Conclusions

Before leaving the store, spend a few minutes reviewing everything you saw in the store and reach some conclusions. Determine the problems that exist for your products in the store and note opportunities for your products that are being missed.

Step 7—Record Your Observations and Conclusions

Writing down or recording your observations and conclusions about each store is important if you are to make valid generalizations about in-store conditions in a market. Even with a good memory, it is difficult to remember specific in-store conditions after you have visited more than a few stores. The store survey form presented in the practice exercise on the next page is an example of a tool for recording in-store observations.

PRACTICE EXERCISE: Conclusions from an In-Store Survey

Outline the conclusions you would reach from the information recorded on the store-survey form presented below:

STORE SURVEY FORM

MARKET _VALLEY JUNCTION_   MANAGER _N. ROBERTS_   PURPOSE _____

STORE TYPE
P—Package   C—Convenient
F—Food   B—Bar-Lounge
D—Drug   O—Other

FLOOR DISPLAY CONCERNS
1. Well Located   4. Header Card
2. Right Size   5. Clean & Neat
3. Priced   6. One Product/Group

SHELF CONCERNS
1. Enough Space   4. Line Together
2. Competitive Distribution 5. Arranged for Trade Up
3. Good Shelf Location   6. Point of Sale

NAME & ADDRESS OF STORE	TYPE OF STORE	* FLOOR DISPLAYS 1	2	3	4	5	6	Comments	* SHELF REGULAR/SPECIALTY 1	2	3	4	5	6	Comments	DISTRIBUTION LACKING	COMPETITIVE ACTIVITY
1. HOWARD'S 3RD + MARKET	PACKAGE													√	BOTTOM SHELF SPEC. COS	REGULAR GALLONS	HAS THE WINE BUSINESS ALL PLUS OTHER COMPETITION — OUR DISTRIBUTOR
2. SAFETY 3RD + POLK	FOOD		√	√	√	√		HAS EVERY PRODUCT ON DISPLAY		√	√	√	√	√	BOTTOM SHELF STK. ODS	RECENTLY DISCONTINUED FIFTHS	
3. 11-7 3RD + NEVER	FOOD									√	√	√	√	√	BOTTOM SHELF 20-70 SEGMENT		
4. SAMSONS 23RD + VINE	FOOD	√			√	√		NO HEADER CARD		√					DETINED GALLO AND BOTTOM SHELF	NO FIFTHS HALF-GALLONS	
5. SAFETY 23RD + VINE	FOOD	√		√	√	√		HAS EVERY PRODUCT ON DISPLAY		√	√	√	√		BOTTOM SHELF		
6. GO-GO 3RD + NEVER	FOOD														OVER THE DELI CASE NO SPEC. WINE	NEEDS ALL ON THE 20-70 SPECIALTY WINES	
7. SAMSONS 24TH + VINE	FOOD	√		√	√			NO HEADER CARD		√	√	√	√		BOTTLES IN GALLO AND LITTLE SHELF		
8. HARRY'S 25TH + VINE	PACKAGE													√	LITTLE SHELF SPEC. COS	REGULAR LINE HALF-GALLONS	

* Place a √ if standard is met, leave blank if it is not met.

Conclusions Reached: _____

RECORDS

Since sales organizations exist to sell products, it is a rare organization that does not have company case sales records. The simplest records consist of manually tabulated records of total cases sold. More typical today are the computer printouts which contain basic sales information like:

- Case sales by brand by size by account.
- Case sales by brand by size by territory.
- Case sales by brand by size as compared to goal or forecast.
- Percentage of increases or decreases by brand by size.

Records of In-Store Conditions

Since many of the consumer product sales team goals are merchandising goals, there is an increasing trend to keep records of in-store accomplishments. Examples of this type of record would be: (1) the number of accounts with floor displays, (2) the number of accounts with products on reach-level shelves, (3) the number of accounts featuring a product in their newspaper ads, (4) the number of accounts with shelf space gains.

Some companies turn to outside research organizations for information on in-store conditions for their products. Two of the more prominent organizations are SAMI and Nielsen. SAMI reports are based on shipments from chain store or wholesale warehouses to stores. They contain information on distribution, sales by brand and size and promotional case sales. Nielsen reports are based on in-store audits. They contain information on out-of-stocks, competitive and private label activities and percentage shares.

Industry Reports

Industry reports are generated from the records of publicly held companies and in some instances from tax payments. These reports can be used to interpret team sales trends. For example, a decrease in the sales of a brand are of less concern in a decreasing industry category than they are in an increasing industry category.

Using the Records

Whether the records are manual or computer produced, they are only as good as the use that is made of them. The records are created to give you information about sales activity on your team. The information must be evaluated before it can be used to direct team sales activity.

Learning how to use the information available from these records to spot trouble and uncover opportunities is one of the more difficult skills for action-oriented sales managers to acquire. A sales trainer I know once seriously suggested that new sales managers be denied access to all company records for the first six months on the job. It was felt that forcing new sales managers to generate their own records would help them develop an appreciation for what the company does for them. Probably a more reasonable approach would be to learn how to use the company records one at a time. This approach allows you to study each record and prevents you from being overwhelmed.

MEASURING AND EVALUATION

Measuring lets you know whether the goals you planned to reach are being reached. When you determine that a goal is not being reached, you must do something to see that the goal is met. Before deciding on what needs to be done, the cause of the problem must be determined. Determining the cause of the problem, determining the reason why the goal is not being met is what evaluating is all about.

EVALUATING

Once a problem has been spotted, the search for the cause should begin. Something has gone wrong, and the cause of the problem must be found before a solution can be developed. More characteristically, sales managers begin the search for solutions without identifying the cause of the problem. For example, a meeting is called as soon as it becomes evident that a floor display program is failing. A special sales crew is set up when distribution for new products is far below set goals. An incentive is offered to boost sales when sales of a brand begin to sag. All of these are examples of solutions developed without defining the cause. The danger in developing solutions without determining the cause is that the problem may go unsolved. Direction can be given which will not lead to sales goals.

FINDING THE CAUSE

The cause of most sales problems can be found by systematically examining all of the information available. A system for doing this is presented below:

The Cause Finding Process:
- State the goal not being met
- Question the available information
- Develop possible causes
- Test possible causes

State the Goal Not Being Met

Identify the goal or goals not being met. This should include the product, the size, the territories, the type of account and the type of goal not being met. For example: The case sales for the small sizes of your product have decreased by 1,000 cases in the last month. The team goals were to have a 100 case increase. By stating the product, the size and the time frame, you can focus on the relevant information. As an example, sales of small sizes become the focus of your search for a cause.

Question the Information

There are six fundamental questions that should be asked when you are searching for the cause of a problem. They are:

1. *Is the total business up or down or is it just one of a few products?*
2. *Are sales up or down in all areas or just a few?*
   - Urban-Residential
   - College Area
   - Inner City Area
   - Suburban Area
   - Recreation Area
3. *Are sales up or down in all types of accounts or just a few?*
   - Chain or Large Accounts
   - Independent Accounts
4. *Where did the business go?*
   - To a competitive product
   - To another size of the same product
   - To another product produced by us
   - To a product priced differently than ours
5. *When did the change first occur?*
6. *How much have sales changed?*
   - More than can be expected for the season
   - More than last year at this time

The answers to these six questions suggest possible causes for most of the sales problems you will face.

For example:

1. Business is up for all products and sizes except for the problem product.
2. Sales of small sizes are down only in the inner-city areas.
3. Sales of small sizes are down in independent accounts not in the chains.
4. Sales increases of small sizes of a similar competitive product seem to be occurring.

5. Up until a month ago, sales of the small sizes were on target.
6. The sales decrease of 1,000 cases cannot be explained by seasonal fluctuations.

Develop Possible Causes

The cause of most problems is usually the result of some unanticipated change. The change somehow prevents the sales representative from reaching the goals they set. These unanticipated changes suggest possible causes for the problem.

Using this approach, possible causes for the small size decrease could be: (1) last month's small size sales contest, (2) a new inner-city sales representative, (3) the major inner-city independent account went bankrupt, (4) shelf space for small sizes has been lost to one of our new brands.

Each of these is a possible cause that could explain the 1,000 case drop in the sale of small sizes. A consideration of each of these possible causes should lead us to the cause.

Test Possible Causes

When you feel you know the cause of the problem, test your conclusion. If it is the real cause it should be able to account for the existence of the problem. Possible causes can be tested by using the formula: If _____ is the cause, does this explain why this goal was not met and others were met?

For example: If the bankrupt account is the cause, would it explain why there is a 1,000 case drop? No, they only bought 200 cases of the small sizes last year. If last month's small size contest is the cause, would it explain the drop of 1,000 cases and a drop in the inner city alone? Probably it could.

By testing each of the possible causes that are derived from an examination of the available information, it is possible to develop the most probable cause. It is a matter of checking each cause against all of the available information.

MEASURING, EVALUATING, DIRECTING

Measuring sales goal attainment lets you know what is happening on your sales team and brings problems to the forefront. By evaluating the information available, the cause of the problem can be isolated. The cause will suggest the direction that needs to be given.

The direction given is obviously a matter of motivation. Remembering how to get people to do what you want them to do is essential to effective sales team direction.

DIRECTING

If everything is happening as planned, you do not need to alter the directions to your sales team. If a problem has been discovered, new direction needs to be given. Directing consists of deciding what to do to see that goals and objectives are reached.

Individual or Team

In some situations, the problem exists with one or a few team members. In these situations, only they need to be re-directed. In situations where the goals are not being reached by all of the team members, a team oriented solution is needed.

DECIDING ON THE DIRECTION

When sales goals and merchandising objectives are not being met, something must be done to correct this situation. The sales manager's task is to decide what to do.

Let's say, for example, due to the increase in your competitor's cooperative advertising contribution, the number of retail ads your team has been able to sell is far below the forecast. As a team leader, you must decide what to do. What can you do? What are your options?

Options are almost limitless, unless you force yourself to realize that the directions you give are limited by the resources available. Options are further limited by the fact that the direction given should lead to goal attainment without disrupting other team sales activity. There are about four things to keep in mind when you are formulating plans for corrective action:

Deciding On Corrective Action:

- Assign the goal a priority
- Determine the resources available
- Think about alternative directions
- Decide on one and use it.

Goals and Priorities

The direction taken must be compatible with all of the other goals of the team. Assigning the goal a priority when compared with all of the other goals puts the goal in perspective. For example: Assigning the goal of gaining retailer ad support a priority rating of 9 on the team, puts the goal in perspective. It is an important goal, but not a top priority goal. The direction given to reach the goal as a result must not interfere with the more important, higher priority goals of the team.

Resources Available

As stated before, if the personnel, money and materials available are unlimited almost any goal can be reached with almost any solution. Most goals, however, must be reached with limited resources. For example, the solution to the problem of lack of retailer ad support might be to increase the contribution to match that of your competitor. If the funds are not available, a different solution would have to be sought.

Think about Alternatives

In problem situations, many managers are convinced that doing anything is better than doing nothing. As a result, they give direction without really thinking through the alternatives that are available to them. A thoughtful consideration of alternatives and the consequences of using each significantly improves the chances of success for the corrective action taken. In our example, some of the alternatives that should be considered are:

1. Increase your cooperative advertising contribution.
2. Sell the retail ads yourself.

3. Re-train your salespeople to sell retail ads.
4. Bring in a sales crew to sell the ads.
5. Express your concern to members of the sales team, suggest they increase their efforts.

Decide and Do

Consider each alternative in light of the goals you want to reach and the resources available and then decide what to do. If an alternative costs more or requires more resources that you have, it has to be eliminated. You must then consider one of the remaining alternatives and direct the individual or team accordingly.

PRACTICE EXERCISE: Deciding on Corrective Action
for a Failing Program

Three solutions have been proposed to correct the failing program for Tangello Thud. Choose one of these solutions and explain why you chose the solution.

The Situation

Two weeks after the introduction of a new beverage, Tangello Thud, it is apparent that the program is failing. With two weeks to go the team score is as follows:

- 20 percent of the accounts have floor displays
- 15 percent of the accounts have cold box distribution

Of a team of six people, only one person has reached his goals and he has already reached all of them. The other five salespeople have not reached their floor and cold box goals. At the end of the second week they haven't reached the first week's goals.

The Cause of the Problem

The three experienced salespeople who have not met their goals are just not equipped to make presentations that sell Tangello Thud. They are too accustomed to the slide-in sales which worked with previous beverages. The two new salespeople are just snowed under with the objection—"Not another beverage."

In brief, five of the six salespeople can't sell Tangello Thud.

Unfortunately, you have been assigned a special project and will not be available to work with your people for the next two weeks.

Goals

Floor displays in 60 percent of accounts.
Cold box distribution in 80 percent of accounts.

Resources
   Six salespeople
   $200 limit on expense

Solution #1:   Train salespeople to use a canned presentation with a sales brochure costing about $180.

Solution #2:   Hold a retailer education meeting with passouts, tastings and a speaker. Total cost for meeting—$190.

Solution #3:   Assign the successful Tangello Thud sales representative to work with each sales representative one day in the field. In order to free up the successful sales representative, you would have to hire someone to cover his accounts for a week. His salary for the week would be $160.

Which solution would you choose? _____

_____

Why is this solution the best solution? _____

_____

_____

SUMMARY: CONTROLLING

Controlling sales activity consists of measuring, evaluating and directing sales activity on a team. Measuring involves getting information on in-store merchandising accomplishments and case sales which allow you to determine which goals are not being met. Evaluating consists of finding out why the goal is not being met. Once the cause has been determined, something must be done to correct the problem; that is what directing is all about.

QUESTIONS THAT NEED ANSWERS

To be sure that you understand the ideas discussed in this chapter, answer the following questions.

1. Control consists of:
   a) measuring, problem solving, directing.
   b) getting information, evaluating, correcting.
   c) getting information, problem solving, directing.
   d) all of these.

2. Planning and controlling are:
   a) interconnected.
   b) totally different.
   c) easily confused.
   d) part of the same process.

3. A source of information used to control sales activity is:
   a) consumer acceptance reports.
   b) sales representative activity reports.
   c) retail sales reports.
   d) product position reports.

4. An information retrieval form should be designed for:
   a) ease of completion.
   b) completeness of information.
   c) manager's convenience.
   d) clerical accuracy.

5. The method for choosing representative stores for a survey which requires a list of all the stores in a market is:
   a) ride and pick.
   b) random selection.
   c) focus picture.
   d) list and map.

6. Most basic company sales records include:
    a) case sales by brand.
    b) production costs.
    c) comparative profits.
    d) competitive case sales.

7. A sales manager who spots a problem should immediately:
    a) find the cause.
    b) develop a solution.
    c) ask for help.
    d) all of these.

8. One of the six fundamental questions that a sales manager should ask when he faces a problem is:
    a) are the figures right?
    b) have trade loyalties shifted?
    c) is the sales force trained?
    d) where did the business go?

9. Directing consists of:
    a) goal setting.
    b) evaluating information.
    c) thinking before acting.
    d) taking corrective action.

10. Resources consist of available:
    a) promotion monies.
    b) sales help.
    c) POS material.
    d) all of these.

If you made the following choices, you should feel that the ideas discussed are yours: 1d, 2a, 3b, 4a, 5d, 6a, 7a, 8d, 9d, 10d.

Chapter 9

Communicating with the Sales Team

WORDS, WORDS, WORDS

"It should be clear from the memo I sent you ..."

"You agreed to do it when we talked on the telephone last week."

"Where were you when we discussed that subject at our last meeting?"

"In your last report you said ..."

The quotations above are expressions of some of the frustrations sales managers experience in communicating with their sales representatives. Words are exchanged, but somehow the messages get lost.

Why should this be? Sales representatives are communicators by profession, and sales managers, because of their experience, should be equally professional communicators. There are certainly some similarities between communicating with a customer and communicating with sales team members, but there are also some important differences. The telephone is used more frequently, meetings are used to communicate, memos are used to give direction, information is exchanged through the use of written reports. Clearly, sending and receiving messages from and to members of a sales team is not the same as face-to-face customer communication.

COMMUNICATING DEFINED

In order to be sure that we are communicating about communicating, it might be well to define the term. *Communication is the process of sending and receiving messages.* The message may consist of ideas, feelings, thoughts, or attitudes. The most commonly used form of communication is personal, face-to-face talking and listening.

Communication Consists of:

- letting a person know how you feel or what you think about something (sending a message)
- listening while another person lets you know how he feels and what he thinks about something (receiving a message)

THE FIELD SALES MANAGER AS A COMMUNICATOR

A Field Sales Manager sends messages through the use of the telephone and in face-to-face conversations. He also writes letters and memos. Messages are received in much the same way.

In order to improve your skill as a communicator, six important rules for effective speaking and writing have been developed. Once these have been presented, effective ways of improving your listening and reading comprehension will be presented.

SIX RULES FOR EFFECTIVE SPEAKING AND WRITING

Communication with members of your team can be made assured if you follow the six rules presented below:

Rule 1: Think the message through.
Rule 2: Open with words that will gain attention.
Rule 3: Clarify what you want to discuss at the beginning.
Rule 4: Personalize the message.
Rule 5: Anticipate objections and answer them.
Rule 6: Repeat and close with key points.

Rule 1: Think the Message Through

Before you begin to speak or write, stop and think. What do you want to say? What are you trying to accomplish with the message you are about to send? What do you want the person receiving the message to do as a result of your message? Know what you want to say before you start talking or writing.

If the manager writing the memo, mentioned in the introduction, had taken only a few minutes to think through the message he wanted to send, the sales representatives would have known exactly what they were to do.

One suggestion that will help you think through the message before you deliver it is to write out the message before you dictate it. By writing out the memo, letter or speech, you are forced to think through your message and give it logical order and meaningful clarity. Seeing the message in writing makes it easier to insure that your message is clear, complete and concise.

Rule 2: Open with Words That Will Gain Attention

Whenever you address another person, you are competing for attention. You must compete with the thoughts someone was thinking before you addressed him. He must switch his attention from his thoughts to your message. This may involve some effort on his part and some skill on yours to get through to him.

Suppose you meet one of your sales representatives late in the afternoon about the time he usually heads for home. He is thinking of one thing, going home. Before he leaves his territory, you want to meet with him and tell him about the new credit policy the company has just adopted.

In order to get his attention, you could ask, "Did you hear about the new credit policy we're installing today?" Or you could say, "Don't be surprised if there is some confusion tomorrow when you call in your orders. We expect some confusion because we're installing a new credit system."

Or you might even begin with, "We've all been concerned about the orders that have to be sent back to the warehouse when customers don't have the cash or credit to pay for them. Now, we're going to do something about them. We're installing a new credit policy tomorrow."

The first attention-getter is an involving question; the second, a startling statement; the third, a statement that reflects both a familiar problem and something of common interest. These are the three methods of appealing to someone's interest and gaining his attention.

In many instances, just mentioning a person's name may be enough to gain his full attention. However, if that doesn't work, try one of the other techniques:

- Ask an involving question.
- Make a startling statement.
- Cite a familiar problem.
- Mention something of common interest.

Rule 3: Clarify What You Want to Discuss at the Beginning

To make the message clear, state your topic, what the message is about, at the beginning. For example, in starting a conversation about new store call procedure, you might say, "Fred, I'd like to talk with you about the new store call procedure." If you were writing instead of talking, you would start by writing what your subject is about at the top of the memo or letter. For example, "Subject: New Store Call Procedure." Making the subject of your message clear at the beginning helps the listener or reader focus his attention on the central idea.

Rule 4: Personalize the Message

In order for a message to mean anything to the person receiving it, it must be personalized. This means that the person listening to or reading it must be able to apply what you say to himself. Three ways to personalize a message are:

- Use names whenever possible.
- Use words that are commonly used by receivers.
- Cite examples that your receivers can relate to.

Names, words, and examples help bring the message across more effectively. Using a person's name in a conversation with him or using both his name and title in your writing will naturally make the message more personal. "As you know, Greg, there are three parts to the pricing information form" is a more personal statement for Greg than simply, "As you know, there are three parts to the pricing information form." Adding his name gives your message a personal touch. You are saying, "This message was personally designed for you." Similarly, in writing a memo to the sales representatives on the team with chain headquarter responsibility you can identify the position as: key account sales representatives.

Familiar words which you use in your everyday conversations should be used in your spoken and written communications with your salespeople. Some sales managers make the mistake of trying to use words which suggest they have a superior vocabulary. The result usually is lack of clarity and a muddled message. Differences in background and geography will affect how you word your message. Listen to the everyday conversation of your salespeople, and use their expressions and vocabulary in your communications with them. Explaining the chain store order procedure to a person who has never worked in a chain store obviously requires a different message and different words than it does to an experienced chain sales representative. Urban territory management to a sales representative of rural background requires a different message than it does to a city-born sales representative.

Rule 5: Anticipate Objections and Answer Them

Try to anticipate any possible objections to what you are saying or writing. Be ready to answer them if they come up in a conversation or a memo. Many objections are really questions which are asking for more information. If you make an effort to explain your position and the reasons for your decisions, your speaking and writing style will be clearer and more effective.

Suppose you want to convey the message, "Daily reports will be completed daily and sent daily." In instructing the sales representatives to do this you should anticipate the objection, "He won't read them until the end of the week anyway." "Getting to the post office takes away from my selling time." In preparing the message, you should anticipate these objections and answer them before they are raised. You might point out that while you are sometimes in the field, and unable to read the reports daily, you do on occasion have to answer to your boss about the daily activities of your sales representatives, therefore . . . Another point that could be made is that daily reports prevent surprises at the end of the week and can signal a need for help. Anticipate objections and answer them.

Rule 6: Repeat and Close with Key Points

A very successful communicator who was managing people yet spoke poor English was asked why his messages were generally so well understood. His answer was: "I tell 'em what I'm going to tell 'em, I tell 'em the message, and then I tell 'em what I told 'em." He repeated the key points of his message time after time in different ways and in various contexts until it became clear. The technique of repeating key points does not mean that you should say exactly the same thing in the same way over and over. It does mean, however, that you should say what you want to say, illustrate it with examples, and then rephrase the message in other words. For example, you want one of your sales representatives to make more effective use of visual selling sheets. You might say, "The use of a sales sheet is to study it before you try to use it. Get the message clear in your mind first. Then use it like a cue-card—hold onto it, customize it and use it to review the retailer benefits. To put it in simpler words, study it, hold onto it, customize it and use it to review the benefits."

Repeating the message makes it clearer and helps build understanding. No matter how many times the key points of the message are repeated, try to close with a repetition of the key points. Repeat, repeat, repeat and close with a repeat of the key points!

PRACTICE EXERCISE: Evaluating Communications

Using the six rules of communication, evaluate the report sales manager Williams sent to his boss.

TO: GENERAL SALES MANAGER: **Helen Martin**

FROM: DISTRICT SALES MANAGER: **Carl Williams**

SUBJECT: **TEAM TARGETS AND THINGS IN THE WAY**

Unfortunately, this report is late as a consequence of my recent extra work in executing the training program as specified in my job description of a new salesman. The team has been hard at work on this program as they usually are. Some of the people have made gigantic and spectacular gains in their shelves from working this program and sales are increasing from their concentrated, unparalled efforts.

Of the 60 target accounts involved in this program we have gained space in 20. Not bad (in my humble opinion) for a two-month plan. However, we plan to hit bigger targets in the ensuing month. Maybe 25 more, maybe more if I have some time to direct the bombers, but hell, even with little help from the team's commander-in-chief, we gained a total space target of:

70 Feet Lineal

All six salespeople had effective results using our space gaining plan and are convinced it can work in all areas with any salesperson under any conditions. Two points seem directive in this very special program. Use the visual support tools and talk dynamite sales volume in terms of overall cases. I will report on next quarter's results next quarter. By the way, team sales are up 15 percent because of this plan, and the team gained 20 new placements. How about that for being on target?

FACE-TO-FACE CONVERSATIONS

As we pointed out before, most sales managers are at their best in face-to-face conversations. Nevertheless, something can be gained by questioning. Ask yourself each of the questions listed below.

1. Do you look for the assumptions in statements that others make? You should. For example, if your secretary says that your bookkeeping system won't work for her, try to determine why. What assumptions is she making?

2. Do you use the same word to respond to every statement or question? You shouldn't. Repeating the same word, whether it's "super," "great," "dynamic," or "grand," puts your sincerity in doubt.

3. Do you pay attention to your eyes and your hands when you are speaking? You should. The look in your eye and the way you hold your hands are two of the actions that speak louder than words.

4. Do you adjust your rate of speaking to the individual you are speaking with? You should. Speaking too quickly simply confuses a person who is slow. On the other hand, speaking too slowly annoys the speedier person. If you stop occasionally and ask for feedback, you will be able to tell if your listener is with you or behind you.

5. Do you tend to answer questions before the question has been completed? You shouldn't. The tendency to listen to a few words and then give an answer is a dangerous habit. Not only will you frequently mistake the question, but you will frustrate your questioner. What's more, people will have more confidence in your responses if they know you have heard the whole question. Snap answers do not satisfy questioners.

6. Do you control your desire to over-impress others? You should. If you don't you are apt to give a thirty-minute lecture when a three-word statement is appropriate. Besides, you may intimidate and frustrate your listener, thereby blocking effective communication.

7. Can you gauge how strongly a person feels about something he says? You should be able to. The tone of the person's voice will

tell you when he is only mildly convinced of something. On the other hand, when there is no question in his mind, it may be an important clue for you to know.

8. Do you make it a point to use the person's name frequently in your conversation? You should. Using the person's name at the beginning of the conversation is not enough. When you use the person's name, you personalize the message so it can be received more favorably.

9. Do you show respect for the other person's opinion, even if you think he is wrong? You should. A good phrase to use is, "You may be right, but why do you feel that way?" A question like this shows that you will consider an answer if it proves correct or possible, and at the same time encourages the other person to reexamine the reasons for his own opinion.

10. Do you accept what people say as their final opinion? You shouldn't. Sometimes a person will make a tentative statement merely to feel you out. At other times, initial opinions will change after you've discussed the matter. Leave the conversation open to a change of heart.

Face-to-Face Conversations will be Effective if you:
- Look for assumptions.
- Avoid repeating the same response word.
- Watch your hands and eyes.
- Adjust your rate of speaking.
- Listen to questions before answering them.
- Control your desire to over-impress.
- Gauge how strongly a person feels.
- Use the other person's name frequently.
- Respect the other person's opinion.
- Never accept the other person's opinion as final.

THE KNACK OF GIVING ORDERS

The rules for giving orders are basically the same as those for all speaking and writing. However, how an order is conveyed is particularly important in how it is received.

There are a number of ways in which orders can be given. One way is to *command* that something be done. "Sell this shelf change now!" is an example of a command. While commands are sometimes necessary, they can be abrasive and often cause resentment. It is usually better, therefore, to make requests and give suggestions.

Requests are direct but respectful statements of need or responsibility. "I'd like to see you making your store calls on schedule" is such a statement. *Suggestions* are hints that something should be done. "Could we see how this retailer will respond to a suggested shelf change?" Such ways of ordering are generally given to people who are particularly sensitive and who can carry out their jobs without detailed instructions.

Generally, people appreciate and respond to direct but thoughtful prodding. If you are careful to follow the rules for effective speaking, this kind of order will work best.

TALKING BY TELEPHONE

Most field sales managers communicate frequently by telephone. Whether speaking to your boss at headquarters or to one of your sales representatives, the telephone rules listed below will help make your calls clearer and more effective.

Telephone Rules:

1. Think before you call.
2. Identify yourself.
3. Make the purpose known.
4. Use only when urgent.
5. Call back when necessary.

Take time to think your message through before you dial. If you have several points to cover, jot down a few notes to help you remember to cover them all. Identify yourself by name as soon as the other person answers the phone, and make the purpose of your call clear from the start. That way, they will be tuned in to the substance of the message.

Since retailers usually resent telephone calls for sales representatives in stores, telephone calls should be made only when the message is urgent. The same is true for early morning and evening telephone calls at home: only when the message can't wait.

Try not to ask for information that requires a lengthy search while you wait on the phone. It's a waste of everyone's time. Instead, after you call the person, either ask them to call you back when they have the information you need, or indicate a time when you will call them. If you follow these rules, you will make the telephone an effective management tool for your use.

COMMUNICATING THROUGH TEAM MEETINGS

Participative team meetings and discussion-oriented training meetings have previously been discussed. The participative and discussion meetings stress the receiving and sending of messages, the two-way communication process in meetings. On occasion, the two-way process will be less important than communicating the action you wish to result from the meeting. This type of meeting is called the action-oriented team meeting. Action-oriented meetings have one purpose and that is to get sales representatives *to do something*. They are the easiest to evaluate. The action-oriented team meeting is successful if the people do what you want them to do and a failure if they don't do what you want them to do.

There is a tendency today to characterize the inspirational type of sales meeting as outdated. Showmanship is a questionable virtue in the opinion of these people. Information, they claim, is enough. Tell them what to do and they'll do it. Admittedly, there is some truth in this opinion, but it denies the importance of the human emotions. People have hearts as well as heads and inspiring is as important as informing. There is probably no better way to get people to do what you want them to do than to get them excited about it.

The six rules for effective communication mentioned earlier in this chapter will assure that you make it clear what you want the sales representatives to do. A bit of showmanship will make the message emotionally appealing and result in better field performance.

A simple formula for conducting action-producing meetings is M-E-E-T. *M*uster attention by doing something different. *E*ncourage interest—use audio-visual support whenever possible: slides, movies, tapes and charts. *E*xcite action—point out the benefits to them. *T*op off with a high positive note. Sum it up with a clear statement of what you want them to do and end the meeting with an optimistic statement of the positive results of their actions.

**PRACTICE EXERCISE: Planning an Inspiring,
Action-Oriented Meeting**

Answer the Following Questions About an Upcoming Action-oriented
Meeting you Plan to Hold.
1. State below what you want the team members *to do* as a result
   of the meeting:

   _____

   _____

2. How do you plan to introduce the topic?

   _____

   _____

3. What techniques do you plan to use to make the message inspiring as well as informative?

   _____

   _____

Complete the Following Agenda

TOPIC	TECHNIQUE/TOOLS	TIME
_____	_____	____
_____	_____	____
_____	_____	____
_____	_____	____
_____	_____	____
_____	_____	____
_____	_____	____
_____	_____	____
_____	_____	____
_____	_____	____
_____	_____	____

MESSAGE SENT—MESSAGE RECEIVED?

How can you be sure that the message sent is understood and received correctly? Obviously the more effectively you use the six rules, the more certain you can be that the message you send will be the same message that is received. To make sure that the receiver gets the right message, you should always ask for feedback or for a restatement of what he has heard or read. This is the best way to insure that your message comes across. Encourage your listener or reader to describe in his own words what you have said.

The following example should make clear why it is so important to get feedback.

Sales Manager: "Selling the floor program to your top five accounts is very important. Better give it your full attention." (This statement could be interpreted by the sales representative to mean: "Put everything else aside until this project is completed." Or it could mean: "Be particularly thorough in handling this project.")

Sales representative: "You want me to drop everything else until I get this done?" (Here, the sales representative feeds back his understanding of the message.)

The message the manager wanted to convey was: "Pay attention to this project. Don't treat it lightly." Through feedback, it was clear that a different message was received. Unless you ask for feedback or restatement of what you say and write, you have no way of knowing what message was actually received.

WRITTEN COMMUNICATION

Like speaking, writing also requires that you follow the six basic rules of communication. Again, they are:

- Think the message through.
- Use written words to get the receiver's attention.
- Write your message clearly, and clarify from the very beginning what you want to say.

- Personalize the message where possible, and tailor your message to your receiver.
- Anticipate objections and answer them.
- Repeat or summarize your key points.

THE MESSAGE REPLY FORM

Message reply forms speed up message sending and receiving by encouraging brief messages. This message reply form is prepared in triplicate. Two copies are sent to the receiver. He keeps one and returns the other to the manager. The third copy is usually filed.

Some features of the message reply form are:

- It forces you to make your message brief and to the point. It is purposely designed with limited space for this reason.
- It provides the receiver with an easy way to respond. He simply records the answer in the reply section of the original memo and returns it to the sender.
- It is particularly useful in situations where secretarial service is limited. The memo can be easily handwritten.
- It can be purchased from supply houses with three carbon copies. This gives everyone a copy and everyone a record.

MESSAGE Date / /	REPLY Date / /
Signed	Signed

DOES ANYBODY READ THE BULLETIN BOARD?

In situations where sales representatives work out of an office or distribution center, bulletin boards are potentially one of the greatest communication tools. Unfortunately, they are all too frequently neglected. Year-old messages sometimes remain posted on the board long after they are current. Letters and lengthy memos that require ten minutes to read are often prominently displayed. Bulletin boards are effective communication tools only as long as you keep the messages posted on the board current and brief.

The easiest way to see that messages are kept current is to insist that all messages posted on the board be dated. No message should be left on the board more than a week.

Keeping messages brief, however, is a bit more difficult. One manager solved the problem by allowing only messages that would fit on a 3 × 5 card to be posted. He recommended that a letter be sent if the employee needed more space than that. While it may be more difficult to write a brief message than a lengthy one, people consent to read brief messages more frequently. Lengthy messages are almost always overlooked.

Remember: Keep messages on bulletin boards brief and current.

CHOOSING YOUR METHOD OF COMMUNICATION

Choosing the best way to send a message depends upon three factors:

- The number of people who need to receive the message.
- The urgency of the message.
- The complexity of the message.

In speaking, you can convey messages through: the telephone, face-to-face conversations and meetings. If your message is meant for one or two people, you obviously do not need to call a meeting. Simple conversations in person or over the phone are adequate. On the other hand, if many people are involved, you will probably not want to repeat your message many times. A meeting, which allows you to convey your message just once to a number of people at the same time, is ideal for conveying information to larger groups.

Urgency is also a factor. Telephoning is probably the fastest method of conveying your message. This is appropriate if the message is a simple one. If the message is complex, however, you may decide to opt for a meeting or conversation, unless time is too pressing.

Personal, face-to-face conversations are valuable for several reasons. First, they allow you to use such visual communication aids as drawings or charts if necessary to explain your ideas. Second, they encourage the listener to ask questions. Third, they allow you to see your listener and to interpret his reactions. Seeing doubt or understanding in your listener's face will help you decide whether or not greater clarification is needed.

In writing, messages can be conveyed through letters or memos. Letters should generally be reserved for messages to fewer people, since they are the most personal form of written communication. If the message is urgent, brief and to a large number of people, memos are the best form of communication.

RECEIVING MESSAGES

So far, the focus has been on building your skills of *sending* messages. An equally important part of communication is *receiving* them. To put it another way, listening and reading are as important in communicating as speaking and writing.

Four Ways to Improve Your Listening Skills

A field sales manager needs to know what's going on in his market. He must be able to understand the messages that both his sales representatives and his boss send to him. This means that to be successful, he must be a good listener, not just a passive listener, but an active one: The following rules can help you improve your skills as a listener.

Four Ways to Improve Your Listening Skills

1. Pay attention to the speaker.
2. Search for the central message.
3. Listen for feeling and meaning.
4. Don't ignore the unpleasant.

Each of these suggestions merits further consideration.

Pay attention to the speaker. You should give your full attention to the person speaking. Fumbling with papers, taking phone calls, and stopping the speaker to do something else that can wait are all examples of poor listening habits. They are also considered rudeness by many people. Unless you pay attention and show respect for the speaker, he is not likely to try to communicate or express himself and his feelings. As a result, you may miss an important message.

Search for the central message. Try to pick out or isolate the basic point the speaker is trying to make. Sometimes this is an easy task, at other times, lengthy digressions and unfamiliar examples make it hard to find the message. Search for the central message, and when you think you have it, state it clearly in your own words, and ask the speaker if this is his point.

Listen for feeling and meaning. Use your skills to get the feeling that is being expressed as well as the meaning. Feelings are frequently the important part of a message. Unless you pay attention to them, you may overlook an important idea. Some speakers directly express their feelings; more typically, they are expressed indirectly. As a result, feelings remain hidden unless they are sought out.

Don't ignore the unpleasant. One of the hardest things in the world to do is to really listen to bad news. The unpleasant just tends to get overlooked, especially when it is presented with other information. If you are aware of this tendency, you can force yourself to pay attention to the bad or unpleasant news, as well as to the good or pleasant.

Practice Makes Perfect

Build these skills in listening by using them the very next time someone speaks to you and every time thereafter. Direct your attention to the speaker, isolate the key point, sense the feeling behind the message and don't ignore the unpleasant.

READING: THE OTHER WAY TO RECEIVE MESSAGES

Most people learn to read in grade school, and use this skill for the rest of their lives without trying to improve it. There are many techniques for improving reading skills. Many cost a good deal of money. However, one of the most effective and most easily mastered methods is the SQ3R method.

The SQ3R Method:

The S stands for Survey.
The Q stands for Questions.
The 3 R's are: read, recite, review.

Survey: The first thing to do when you pick up something to read is to survey the whole thing. Take a look at the headings of the various sections in an article, the summary, and any other organizers. If there are no headings, such as in a letter or memo, survey it to determine the central message.

Question: As you read, question what you read. Ask yourself if you really understand what you are reading. Determine through self-questioning whether you are getting the point.

Read: Read actively. As you read, try to remember key phrases and important definitions. You should study any illustrations such as graphs and tables to increase your understanding.

Recite: The advice is simple: Talk with yourself as you read. Periodically try to recall what you have read and then check it with what you have read.

Review: You may understand something very well as you read it, but unless you systematically review the material periodically as you read, your understanding will decrease significantly.

SUMMARY: COMMUNICATION IS A TWO-WAY AFFAIR

Communication is a two-way affair. The sender must have a receiver to hear or read the message and the receiver must have a sender to speak or write to him or her.

Communication is the process of sending and receiving a message. The six rules for effective speaking and writing are: Think through the message first. Open with words that get attention. Clarify your topic at the beginning. Personalize the message through using names, words, and examples. Anticipate and answer objections. Repeat and close with key points.

Choosing the best way to send a message is also an important factor in communicating. Face-to-face conversations are often warm and personal as compared with written or telephone messages. To be sure your messages are clear, always ask for a restatement or feedback from receivers.

Effective use of the telephone and message reply forms are also important information sources, just as are bulletin board messages that are kept brief and current.

Being an effective manager means being sensitive to receiving as well as sending messages. Paying attention to the speaker, searching for the central message, being sensitive to the feelings conveyed and listening to unpleasant as well as pleasant ideas will all improve your listening skills. Using the SQ3R method will help you improve your reading skills.

One of the field sales manager's most valuable management tools is his ability to communicate with the team. If your success and effectiveness depends on this ability, why not make it A-1?

QUESTIONS THAT NEED ANSWERS

To be sure that you understand the ideas discussed in this chapter answer the following questions.

1. Saying that communication is a two-way affair means it:
   a) involves a sender and receiver.
   b) is limited to two people.
   c) contains two messages.
   d) includes feeling and meaning.

2. Which of the following is a suggested way to get attention?
   a) Scream a lot.
   b) Ask involving questions.
   c) Be wordy.
   d) Use familiar words.

3. To insure that the message sent was received and understood correctly, a manager should:
   a) ask for feedback.
   b) restate the message.
   c) involve the listeners.
   d) repeat key points.

4. The first rule for effective speaking and writing is:
   a) think first.
   b) clarify topics.
   c) use meaningful words.
   d) remember the receiver.

5. The subject of the message should be stated at the top of a memo in order to:
   a) limit the subject.
   b) focus on the subject.
   c) insure reading.
   d) promote understanding.

6. The rule, "Personalize the message," means:
   a) use names.
   b) cite examples.
   c) make use of meaningful words.
   d) all of these.

7. Face-to-face communications can be improved if you:
   a) adjust your rate of speaking.
   b) give the right answers.
   c) let people know what you are talking about.
   d) all of these.

8. Bulletin boards will be read if you:
   a) keep messages current.
   b) personalize the messages.
   c) use simple words.
   d) post letters and memos.

9. Searching for the central message is a:
   a) listening skill.
   b) telephone rule.
   c) communication principle.
   d) passive quality.

10. The summary at the end of the chapter should be:
    a) an introduction to the next chapter.
    b) read with interest.
    c) critically examined for detail.
    d) surveyed before reading a chapter.

If you made the following choices, you should feel that the ideas discussed are yours: 1a, 2b, 3a, 4a, 5b, 6d, 7a, 8a, 9a, 10d.

Chapter 10

Handling People on a Sales Team

PEOPLE AND TROUBLE GO TOGETHER

Science fiction writers have designed work worlds almost totally free of people. In these worlds all work is done by highly dependable, emotionless machines. In this type of work setting there are no people problems. Leaders are simply mechanics. Unfortunately, even in the most highly mechanized telephone based sales organization, people are required. Consequently, people and the problems resulting from their working together must be faced by every field sales manager.

This chapter discusses people problems and how to handle them. This includes: a) grievances and discipline, b) talking with people about emotionally toned issues, c) preventing problems with minority salespeople, d) handling difficult employees, e) solving problems with no apparent cause. If you follow the suggestions for dealing with problems, not only will you reduce dissatisfaction on the team, but you will also make the most productive use possible of your most valuable resource: people.

PROBLEMS INVOLVING RULES AND REGULATIONS

As a team leader you are concerned with getting team members working productively and peacefully together. As a result, rules and regulations are established. Sometimes they are loosely stated; at other times they are quite detailed and set in writing. Rules and regulations are designed to help the team reach its goals. Some rules deal with the responsibilities of the salespeople; others, with the responsibilities of managers. However, everyone is expected to follow whatever rules touch their work lives.

Unfortunately, not everyone follows rules and regulations. Consequently, managers must take responsibility for both listening to employee grievances against management and for establishing punitive measures when employees break the rules.

Handling grievances and disciplining salespeople are two of the more difficult tasks which a field sales manager must perform. The following suggestions for handling people who break rules and regulations should make this part of your job easier.

How to Handle Grievances and Discipline Salespeople

- State the rule involved.
- Examine the purpose of the rule.
- Determine whether the rule
  applies in this situation.
- Rectify the wrong done by
  breaking the rule.
- See that the rule will be followed
  in the future.

In order to see how these suggestions work, let's examine grievances first and discuss discipline second.

GRIEVANCES

A grievance is a complaint from a sales representative that one of the rules or policies for working has been broken by management. The way in which a sales representative expresses his grievance may vary. It can be a casual remark made on a work-with or a more formal statement communicated in private. Regardless of how it is expressed, the important thing is how you as a field sales manager react to the grievance.

One thing for sure is that grievances cannot be ignored. While the procedures for handling grievances vary from company to company, almost all use the five steps in one way or another.

Let's take an example: the performance bonus.

The rule: Bonuses are based on performance the previous month and are paid on the 15th of the following month.

The purpose: To make it clear to sales representatives that sales results are the basis of bonuses and to give administrative people time to calculate performance bonuses.

The situation: Sales representative George complains that it's the 20th of the month and he still hasn't received his bonus check. He further comments that he has heard from the sales representatives that have received their bonus that sales results from last month's special program were not included in calculating the performance bonus.

Rectify the wrong: The sales representative should be issued a check immediately or given an explanation of why his bonus check was not received. If there were circumstances which made an exception in the sales program they should be reviewed with George.

See that the rule will be followed: Review the rule with the administrative people and make it clear to the sales representative that performance bonuses do not include sales from special programs.

In handling grievances be sure to start by stating the rule involved. Many grievances can be solved simply by going over the rule. Then ask the sales representative to state what rule he believes management has violated. Look at the situation yourself and see if you agree. This may involve some interpretation on your part. Then either clarify for the sales representative what the rule is, explaining why it is important, or do whatever is necessary to correct the situation.

Suppose sales representative Mary complains that she is being asked to prepare too many special reports. The rules require a sales representative to promptly answer all reasonable requests for information. Most of the time that means completing daily reports and an occasional special report. However, the rule doesn't specify how many special reports can be requested.

Examine the purpose of the rule. Most rules are originally created in the best interests of both the sales representatives and management. In time, some rules become obsolete. See if the rule you are examining still holds. In this case, special reports are obviously still important but too many requests for special reports are an undue imposition on the sales representative's time. Therefore, you would probably agree with the sales representative and ask that the requests for special reports be reduced.

Often rules are generalizations. As such, they must be interpreted in terms of specific situations. Ask yourself, "Does this rule apply in this situation?" One request in a month for a special report is probably occasional, six special reports probably is more than occasional.

When a rule has been broken by management, whether it is intentional or not, the wrong must be righted. Managers as team leaders should be as willing to follow rules as they are to have their salespeople follow them.

If you err, you should be particularly careful to rectify the mistake. In some cases this may mean offering your salespeople time off, additional pay, or a public apology.

Field sales managers usually follow rules they are familiar with. Occasionally, however, a situation arises in which there is some question regarding the rule. This is usually when they break the rules. Once a rule is clarified and an infringement brought to your attention, you should be particularly careful not to break it again.

Grievances in a Unionized Sales Organization

In a situation where sales representatives are unionized, handling grievances is influenced by a contractual agreement. This agreement or contract specifies to a great extent the rules and regulations and most likely specifies the grievance procedure to be used. While a grievance filed through the union has collective power, the suggestions for handling grievances are equally applicable in union as well as non-union situations. As long as you take the time to read the contract (the rules and regulations), know the union leaders involved with the grievance procedure and take grievances seriously, grievances in unionized sales forces need not be feared.

PRACTICE EXERCISE: Handling Grievances

List below three grievances from salespeople that you have handled in the last month.

1. What was grievance? _____

_____

What did you do about it? _____

_____

_____

2. What was grievance? _____

_____

_____

What did you do about it? _____

_____

_____

3. What was grievance? _____

_____

_____

What did you do about it? _____

_____

Watch for Complaints That Are Symptoms of Bigger Problems

One sales manager reported the following incident:

"Tom, the sales representative in my rural territory, called to complain that the carbon paper on the third copy of the order form was not printing through. My first reaction was, "I can't be worried about that." So I told him I'd send him some new forms. Tom, however, insisted on continuing the conversation. As he talked it became clear that he really wanted to talk about something more important. His real complaint was that he was being neglected. He used the form to express his real concern that he was being neglected and that sales in the rural territory were unimportant to me.

Clearly, if the sales manager had not listened to the complaint, he would not have uncovered the bigger problem, the sales representative's feeling that he was being neglected. Listen to the complaints of the people who work for you. They may be symptoms of bigger, more important problems. Consider all complaints, however insignificant. Discuss them with the sales representative. See if he is actually expressing a bigger issue.

DISCIPLINE

The word discipline involves law and order. It is a force that parents and teachers have over youngsters. It is also a force sales managers have over their sales representatives. The word discipline describes the process a manager uses to correct a worker's breaking of rules. If a manager continually ignores rule breaking by his team members, chances are that the salespeople will no longer follow the rules. For this reason, a team leader cannot ignore rule breaking. In fact, one of his jobs is to see that, in the best interest of the sales organization, his people follow the rules.

When a sales representative breaks the rule, a manager must tell him about it. To insure that the rule will not be broken again, he may want to impose a penalty, although a first warning may be sufficient. In discussions of discipline among field sales managers, penalities usually receive the greatest amount of attention. The real focus, however, should stay on the rules and the purpose of the rules.

The goal of these rules, after all, is to have an efficient and profitable sales team.

Let's take an example: The late Henry Hudson.

The rule: Sales representatives are to be on time for sales meetings.

The purpose: To make the best use of everybody's time.

The situation: Henry consistently shows up for meetings fifteen to thirty minutes late. Although he lives furthest from the meeting place and usually has a last-minute crisis to explain for his tardiness, the rule applies.

Rectify the wrong: A reprimand is probably enough if it's the first time you've brought it to his attention. If you've already discussed the matter with him before, you may have to think of a punishment like a fine for every minute he is late.

The result: Either a prompter Henry or a poorer Henry.

One of the most difficult parts of discipline is to rectify the wrongs done when the rules are broken. An example: Pedro feels obligated to help his retailers stock their shelves. The rules say sales representatives may not stock retailers' shelves. You've spoken to him before, so he understands that he is breaking a rule.

What can you do about it? The penalties you can impose are: 1) fire him, 2) lay him off a day or two, 3) warn him in writing that he faces a layoff or termination, 4) reprimand him in person again. Firing an employee is the ultimate punishment and should be used only when no other alternatives are available. A temporary layoff, however, may be enough to force Pedro to stop breaking the rules. The third alternative, a written warning, might work, but it's a gamble. You are giving him an ultimatum which you must follow through with if he continues stocking shelves. The fourth penalty, simply reprimanding him, hasn't worked in the past, so you can assume that it probably won't work this time either.

Whichever penalty you decide on should be in keeping with correcting the wrong and seeing that the rule will be followed in the future. That is, the punishment should fit the crime and should prevent the worker from breaking the rule in the future.

PRACTICE EXERCISE: Discipline

You have heard that one of your sales representatives, Carl Calmer, is trading product samples with sales representatives from other companies. The rule says that samples are to be used only to solicit business from retailers.

- What do you feel is the purpose of this rule?

_____

_____

- List three possible penalties that could be imposed.

_____

_____

_____

- Which penalty would you impose if a verbal reprimand failed?

_____

_____

_____

- What would you do to see that the rule is followed in the future?

_____

_____

TALKING ABOUT EMOTIONALLY TONED ISSUES

The biggest mistake you can make is to deal with emotionally toned issues as you would a factually based problem. People who have an emotional stake in an issue simply cannot view it objectively.

Examples of such issues might be: Fred, who offends females by constant flirting; Sam, the sloppy dresser; and Oliver, whose raunchy jokes annoy customers.

At 35, Fred still sees himself as the high school heart throb and is unwilling to look at himself as anything but. Sam considers himself a saver and does not like to spend his money on things as insignificant to him as decent clothes. Oliver fails to notice the people who are offended by his raunchy jokes; to him they are funny and he claims that the jokes he tells make him different from the "run of the mill" sales representative. These are examples of emotionally toned issues that must be handled delicately. Thoughtlessly confronting these people could result in real people trouble.

Emotionally toned issues can be dealt with effectively if you remember to keep these things in mind:

Handling Emotionally Toned Issues

- Begin your conversation with something that is related to the issue and has something to do with work.
- Slide into the emotionally toned issue by finding a possible link to work. Use the word because.
- Listen until the person responds emotionally.
- Let the person save face.
- Work out a solution to the problem with the person involved that is mutually agreeable.

Let's see how this system works with the three examples above.

Fred the Flirt

You might start your conversation with Fred by asking him if he finds life at 35 about the same as it was at 25. His response will probably allow you to comment on social life and the number of chances outside of work that allow him to make contacts with people. The discussion can then be steered to the point that flirting is great if you are trying to meet people socially but it can interfere with work when people see you as someone who is constantly "on the make." Wait for Fred to emotionally respond to the confrontation. Admit that not all customers object to his flirting; but since it is so difficult to differentiate between those that like it and those that don't, the rule should be not to flirt with customers or their employees.

Sloppy Sam

The conversation with Sam might begin with a discussion about the external appearances of the stores in his territory. The discussion should allow you to make the point that the store's image is pretty much a matter of what outside people see and that to have a good image a store has to spend money. At the right time, you can then make the point the clothes a sales representative wears shape his image. Clean, neat and sharp clothes create the kind of image that allows a sales representative to sell more than a less impressive image. Let Sam save face by pointing out that not all of the clothes he wears can be criticized but let him know that you expect him to make as much of an investment in his image as he expects his retailers to make in their store's image.

Not So Funny Oliver

The easiest approach to Oliver would be to ask him what the latest jokes on the street are and just listen. The evidence you need will most likely come out in the jokes he tells. This will allow you to ask him if he ever finds people who are offended by raunchy jokes. His answer is likely to be yes. The next question would be: Are any of your customers offended? Encourage him to think through the jokes he tells and to resist telling jokes to any of his customers that will offend any of them. This should result in an elimination of the not so funny, raunchy jokes.

Emotionally toned issues are not easy to talk about. As a consequence, many managers of sales teams try to ignore them completely. Team leadership requires that you face these issues; focus on the work implications of the behavior, expect the sales representative to respond emotionally and let him save face and develop a mutually agreeable solution. Not dealing with these emotionally toned issues only creates bigger more difficult to solve people problems.

PRACTICE EXERCISE: Talking over an Emotionally Toned Issue

    Choose an emotionally toned issue that exists on your team. State the issue and then outline the conversation that you will have with the person about the issue.

The emotionally toned issue: _____

_____

Begin with: _____

_____

_____

Because: _____

_____

_____

His anticipated response is: _____

_____

_____

Face saving statement: _____

_____

_____

Solution: _____

_____

PREVENTING PROBLEMS WITH MINORITIES

Since there are an increasing number of salespeople who are members of minority groups, you should pay particular attention to the way you handle them. Generally, sales representatives who are members of minority groups should be handled the same way as non-minority sales representatives. Problems with minority sales representatives usually result from the fact that they feel they are not being treated equally. Examples of problems that can develop with minority salespeople because they feel they are not being treated equally are: a black sales representative's request for a suburban territory is denied. A female sales representative is not sent for management training. An over-40 worker is not given any of the new big case accounts.

What Is a Minority?

A minority group usually refers to a group of people who are not white, not male, not Anglo-Saxon, not under 40 and not physically fit. Females are members of a minority group. So are all people over 40. And so are Blacks, Jews, Chinese and Greeks. In fact, it is difficult not to belong to some group considered a minority by some people. While some minority groups are more visible than others, almost everyone belongs to one minority group or another.

The Characteristics You Associate with Minorities

The characteristics you associate with a minority group are usually the result of experiences that you or someone you know has had or reported they had with a member of the minority group. For example: If you have a 55-year-old sales representative who is constantly sick and out ill, you might tend to feel that anyone over 50 is a poor risk to hire. If you have a female sales representative who is temperamental and touchy, you might generalize and say that all female salespeople are temperamental and touchy. The minority group takes on the characteristics which rightfully belong only to the individual. Once you begin to view an entire group of people as having these characteristics, you can be said to have prejudices. It is these prejudices which are the root of the problems with minority group members. In order to prevent problems, you must force yourself to recognize all of the characteristics you associate with minority groups and be willing to look at the characteristics of the individual rather than rest with those you associate with the minority group.

Recognize the Characteristics

As a team leader, you should take the time to state in writing the characteristics you associate with the minority groups represented on your team. For example, black people are . . . Once stated, you can examine your feelings, challenge them and sometimes even change them simply by recognizing their existence. Whatever the characteristics—good and bad—are that you associate with a minority group, take time to recognize that not every member of the minority group will have these characteristics.

Older sales representatives may be rightly considered more resistant to change; but this is a characteristic that must be established on an individual basis. Asiatics are generally more reserved than non-Asiatics but reservedness is not correctly associated with every Asiatic. Generalizations are made; some of them are appropriate generalizations, others are not. Only a knowledge of the individual sales representative will allow you to differentiate.

THE MESSAGE

Once again, the message: Recognize the characteristics you associate with each minority group, but be willing to discover the individuality of each member of the group.

PRACTICE EXERCISE: Characteristics of Minority Groups

State below the characteristics you associate with each minority group mentioned. Then think of an individual you know who is a member of this group and state which of the characteristics are true of him or her, and how he or she differs.

- Women are: _____

_____

But (Name) _____ is: _____

_____

- Older workers are: _____

But (Name) _____ is: _____

_____

- Blacks are: _____

But (Name) _____ is: _____

- Italians are: _____

But (Name) _____ is: _____

- Homosexuals are: _____

But (Name) _____ is: _____

- Jews are: _____

But (Name) _____ is: _____

- The physically handicapped are: _____

But (Name) _____ is: _____

- Chicanos are: _____

But (Name) _____ is: _____

- Orientals are: _____

But (Name) _____ is: _____

A Button Campaign

A psychologist friend of mind was asked to develop a program for eliminating prejudices toward minorities. The psychologist recommended that a button be printed with the words: "I am an individual!" inscribed on it. He then proposed that each person wear the button for a month. He indicated that the button would bring to everyone's attention the importance of considering the individual. Some group members such as females, Orientals, blacks, and older workers are easy to spot because they are obviously "different" in some way. The button "I am an individual!" brought to everyone's attention the importance of looking beyond the externals.

Don't Be Afraid to Get Burned

In dealing with minority groups and with individual members of minority groups, you may get burned. Some people trust no one outside their group. Your efforts to treat each person as an individual may not always be successful. However, in order to work productively with all of your minority salespeople, you must recognize the characteristics you associate with their group and take time to discover each as an individual.

THREE DIFFICULT PEOPLE TO HANDLE

Managers manage people. And people have feelings. Each person handles these feelings in his or her own individual way. Some of these ways, however, can be difficult or troublesome to you as a manager.

Three kinds of people who pose particular challenges are: the warrior, the complainer, and the know-it-all. Too often, managers who can't deal with such people will let them go rather than try to handle them. However, if you recognize that these people often have valuable assets that they contribute to your operation, you will make every effort to learn to deal with them.

Let's look first at why people behave in challenging, uncomfortable ways. Obviously, no one likes to be difficult. But everyone does have fears: fears of failing, fears of seeming stupid or incapable, fears of not being liked. To hide these fears, or to seem invulnerable to them, a person may behave in a number of ways. He may pick fights. He may complain. He may try to act superior to others. These ways of behaving may seem senseless to you. But to the people who do them, they are important. If many actions are actually cover-ups for hidden fears, how can you approach such issues effectively?

The Warrior

Take the warrior. He seems to be perpetually on the war path. The slightest criticism of his work will set him off. While you would like to keep him on the team because of his hard work, you may not know how to handle him when he intimidates or argues with people. The most important point to remember in dealing with this kind of person is to be firm and strong. Under no circumstances should you act fearful or intimidated by him, since this will indicate to him that his bullying is effective. Once he discovers that you will stand up to his retorts, you will probably find that he no longer gives you trouble.

The Complainer

Another difficult person to handle is the chronic complainer. Again, remember that someone who complains incessantly is probably covering over feelings of inadequacy. His complaints help him take the offensive when he is feeling on the defensive. He is really saying, "If I complain first and loudest, I'll stop other people from complaining about me." The best way to handle this kind of person is to listen to his complaint, show concern, restate the complaint in brighter terms, and go about your business. Don't let his complaints upset or bother you. So long as the complainer doesn't hurt morale or destroy the team, he will be no problem if handled properly.

The Know-It-All

The third kind of difficult person is the know-it-all. Like the warrior and the complainer, he is also acting out of insecurity and anxiety, but in a different way. His protection is to act superior to others by making them feel that he knows more than they do. The best way to handle him is to listen to him with respect. Never try to put him down or make fun of him. You may find that once you get past his delivery, you can actually find some important and useful information in what he says. If you can, you have not only taken advantage of his assets, but made him feel like an important contributing member of the group. As such, he may stop acting so superior so often.

Of course, there may be people who do not respond to your handling skills. These may be people who do not work out anywhere. But most often, with proper handling and understanding, these people can be hard workers and valuable sales team members. If you give some time to learning to deal with them, you will find that your time and understanding of the problem will pay off in the long run.

PEOPLE PROBLEMS WITH NO APPARENT CAUSE

For years, Harvey, our senior sales representative, has had the reputation for working long hours. During the last month, however, he has been watching the clock; starting about thirty minutes late and stopping exactly on time. There is no apparent cause for the change in Harvey's behavior.

One of your customers reports that Andre, his sales representative, told him "take it or leave it." Andre has always been one of the most considerate and polite salespeople you have known. Since there is no apparent cause for the change in Andre's behavior, you are concerned.

The first step in solving a problem is to find the cause. Since the information you now have is not sufficient to give you the answer, you had better collect more information.

Some of the questions you should ask are: When did the problem become apparent? What might have happened to cause the problem? Who might be involved in the problem? What facts might be relevant to the problem? The answers to these and other questions will give you the information you need to determine the cause of the problem. Once a cause has been found, a solution can be developed.

The process looks like this:

1. Ask questions to get more information about the problem.
2. Use the information to determine the cause of the problem.
3. Develop a solution to the problem based on your knowledge of the cause.

Let's see what happens to the problem with Harvey.

1. When did Harvey start cutting his hours? One month ago.
2. What happened one month ago that might have caused the change? His best friend was terminated because of improper accounting of expense monies.
3. Who is involved in the problem? Harvey, you and perhaps the friend.
4. What does the friend have to say about your company? The friend feels he was not fairly treated.
5. What does Harvey have to say? He admits that he has cut back on his work hours but he points out that he's giving the company exactly what they pay for and nothing more.

Now that you recognize the reason for Harvey's behavior, you can sit down with him and work out a solution.

As far as Andre is concerned, you might ask:

1. Why did Andre tell the customer to "take it or leave it"? As far as you can tell the customer did nothing to provoke him.
2. Did anything occur in the territory other than at the account that may have caused Andre to change his behavior? On inquiry you might find that the customer that Andre calls on just before the account from which you received the complaint has been taking advantage of Andre. It is possible the Andre felt taken advantage of and that he expressed his resentment on his next call. The solution is an apology to the customer from Andre and some help from you in resolving his feelings of being taken advantage of.

Before you try to solve any problem without an apparent cause, you must search for information. The information will suggest a cause and a solution. People and their problems are worth the effort required to solve them. Like it or not, as a team leader your salespeoples' work is your problem.

PRACTICE EXERCISE: Solving Problems with No Apparent Cause

On the lines below, outline a problem that you are having with one of your employees that has no apparent cause, answer the questions related to it and see if you can find a solution.

The problem is: _____

_____

When did the problem first occur? _____

Who is involved? _____

What happened before the problem first occurred that might account for it? _____

_____

How frequently does problem occur? _____

What are some possible causes of the problem? _____

_____

Who should you talk to about the matter? _____

What solutions do you propose for the problem? _____

_____

SUMMARY: PEOPLE PROBLEMS

You may notice that there are no recommendations for solving marriage problems, alcoholic anxieties or psychological disturbances. This type of problem is clearly beyond the skill level of most field sales managers. If the people problem does not affect work performance it's a good idea to mind your own business and to stay out of the situation. Giving advice or becoming involved can be both dangerous and destructive.

What kind of people problems are your business? Problems dealing with grievances and discipline. Problems created by emotionally toned issues. Problems related to minority groups. Problems resulting from handling difficult people. These are the problems that are your business and these are the problems that you as a team leader must be willing to deal with. If you follow the suggestions made for handling each type of problem you will have a productive and trouble-free sales team.

QUESTIONS THAT NEED ANSWERS

To be sure that you understand the ideas discussed in this chapter, answer the following:

1. Handling grievances and discipline matters are alike in that both:
   a) deal with rules and regulations.
   b) involve personal matters.
   c) deal with management's perogatives.
   d) involve personal policies.

2. Penalizing an employee by firing him or her:
   a) never does any good.
   b) is less effective than a layoff.
   c) should only be used as a last resort.
   d) none of these.

3. The rule "Do not smoke while working":
   a) is so clear it needs no interpretation.
   b) must be interpreted in specific situations.
   c) is unenforceable.
   d) is incompatible with mental health.

4. A grievance involves:
   a) management responsibilities to workers.
   b) employee responsibilities to management.
   c) both management responsibilities to employee and employee responsibilities to management.
   d) complaints.

5. Which of the following recommendations was not made:
   a) take all complaints seriously.
   b) listen to complaints with an awareness of implications.
   c) consider complaints as if they are symptoms of another problem.
   d) ignore complaints that seem insignificant.

6. The word because is used in talking about emotionally toned issues:
   a) to justify your interest in the issue.
   b) to explain how you see the issue.
   c) to slide into the issue.
   d) to introduce the solution.

7. Which of the groups below would be considered a minority group:
   a) blacks
   b) physically handicapped.
   c) females.
   d) all of these.

8. The basic message of this chapter is: Know the characteristics you assign to minority groups and take time to:
   a) challenge the characteristics.
   b) help the individual.
   c) rid yourself of prejudices.
   d) help the individual.

9. The best way to handle a warrior is to:
   a) get out of his way.
   b) be firm and strong.
   c) embarrass him.
   d) listen then ignore what he says.

10. The formula for solving people problems with no apparent cause is:
    a) determine the cause, ask questions to arrive at a solution.
    b) ask questions, arrive at solutions, determine the cause.
    c) arrive at a solution, ask questions, determine the cause.
    d) ask questions, determine the cause, arrive at a solution.

If you made the following choices, you should feel that the ideas discussed are yours: 1a, 2b, 3b, 4a, 5d, 6c, 7d, 8b, 9b, 10d.